WHY READ AND DISCUSS
THE BOOK OF JOB?

The book of Job is a masterpiece of world literature that occupies a unique place within the Bible. No other biblical book is like it in *form*. It's an extended dialogue between speakers who answer one another in eloquent poetic speeches. (Some works like this are known outside the Bible, but this is the only one in the Bible.) The book of Job is also distinctive in its *language* and *imagery*. The biblical authors draw generally from a shared vocabulary and stock of imagery, but the author of Job goes far beyond this to use a great variety of unique words and images. Finally, while Job pursues the same themes as the other wisdom books of Proverbs, Ecclesiastes, and James—the nature and causes of suffering and blessing in this life—it is also distinctive in the complexity of the *answers* it gives to the problem of suffering that has vexed thoughtful and spiritually sensitive people throughout the ages.

But even though the book of Job is a work of such great beauty and depth, it is more often appreciated as literature by scholars, students, and writers than as Scripture by people of faith. Job is required reading in many college literature programs, and it has inspired modern works such as Franz Kafka's novel *The Trial* and the play *J.B.* by Archibald MacLeish. But believers don't often choose to read and discuss this book together in their small groups, and it's rarely preached about in their worship gatherings.

This may be because believers have difficulty getting past the opening, in which the LORD gives Satan permission to bring horrible loss and suffering into the life of a godly man. This unsettles their confidence in God's fairness and protection. (It may also generate fears that the same thing will happen to them if they get too close!) And even if they do read past the opening, readers often feel as if Job just wrangles endlessly with his friends and then gets browbeaten by God. Seeing this devout man get no sympathy, human or divine, for his undeserved sufferings is simply depressing.

But this is a superficial impression that doesn't do justice to the work's masterful subtlety and depth. In the book of Job there's always more going on than first meets the eye. When readers approach the book with an appreciation for the culture and ideas of the ancient setting in which it was composed, they experience it very differently. They discover that its fearless exploration of some of the most profound questions of human existence provides them with relief, if not joy, by freeing them from the grip of conventional explanations that never quite account for everything. They realize that suffering can have meaning even if its cause and purpose are never known. They recognize that God can be trusted even when he seems to be as much a part of the problem as the solution.

This guide will help you experience the book of Job as the complex, provocative, and liberating work it truly is. You'll understand it in its original setting and appreciate how its parts work together to convey its overall message. You'll recognize how the character of Job actually grows and changes and reaches great insights as the work progresses. You'll share those insights, and you yourself will grow and change in the process. So get some friends together from your church or fellowship or neighborhood and engage this ancient work of profound wisdom. You'll explore questions you never dreamed would come up in a Bible study and never see your world in the same way again.

UNDERSTANDING THE
BOOKS OF THE BIBLE

JOB

Also available in the
UNDERSTANDING THE BOOKS OF THE BIBLE series:

John
Genesis
Wisdom: Proverbs/Ecclesiastes/James
Biblical Apocalypses: Daniel/Revelation
Paul's Journey Letters: Thessalonians/Corinthians/
    Galatians/Romans
Lyric Poetry: Psalms/Song of Songs/Lamentations
Paul's Prison Letters: Colossians/Ephesians/Philemon/
    Philippians/Timothy/Titus

Future releases:

New Covenants: Deuteronomy/Hebrews
Isaiah
Prophets Before the Exile: Amos/Hosea/Micah/Zephaniah/
    Nahum/Habakkuk
Mark

UNDERSTANDING THE BOOKS OF THE BIBLE

JOB

Christopher R. Smith

IVP Connect
An imprint of InterVarsity Press
Downers Grove, Illinois

InterVarsity Press
P.O. Box 1400, Downers Grove, IL 60515-1426
World Wide Web: www.ivpress.com
E-mail: email@ivpress.com

InterVarsity Press® is the book-publishing division of InterVarsity Christian Fellowship/USA®, a movement of students and faculty active on campus at hundreds of universities, colleges and schools of nursing in the United States of America, and a member movement of the International Fellowship of Evangelical Students. For information about local and regional activities, write Public Relations Dept., InterVarsity Christian Fellowship/USA, 6400 Schroeder Rd., P.O. Box 7895, Madison, WI 53707-7895, or visit the IVCF website at <www.intervarsity.org>.

All Scripture quotations, unless otherwise indicated, are taken from the THE HOLY BIBLE, NEW INTERNATIONAL VERSION®, NIV® *Copyright © 1973, 1978, 1984, 2011 by Biblica, Inc.™ Used by permission. All rights reserved worldwide.*

ISBN 978-0-8308-5809-5

Printed in the United States of America ∞

P	20	19	18	17	16	15	14	13	12	11	10	9	8	7	6	5	4	3	2	1
Y	29	28	27	26	25	24	23	22	21	20	19	18	17	16	15	14	13	12

CONTENTS

HOW THESE STUDY GUIDES ARE DIFFERENT

Did you know you could read and study the Bible without using any chapters or verses? The books of the Bible are real "books." They're meant to be experienced the same way other books are: as exciting, interesting works that keep you turning pages right to the end and then make you want to go back and savor each part. The UNDERSTANDING THE BOOKS OF THE BIBLE series of study guides will help you do that with the Bible.

While you can use these guides with any version or translation, they're especially designed to be used with *The Books of the Bible*, an edition of the Scriptures from Biblica that takes out the chapter and verse numbers and presents the biblical books in their natural form. Here's what people are saying about reading the Bible this way:

I love it. I find myself understanding Scripture in a new way, with a fresh lens, and I feel spiritually refreshed as a result. I learn much more through stories being told, and with this new format, I feel the truth of the story come alive for me.

Reading Scripture this way flows beautifully. I don't miss the chapter and verse numbers. I like them gone. They got in the way.

I've been a reader of the Bible all of my life. But after reading just a few pages without chapters and verses, I was amazed at what I'd been missing all these years.

For more information about *The Books of the Bible* and how to use the UNDERSTANDING THE BOOKS OF THE BIBLE series alongside it with your church, visit www.biblica.com/cbe.

For people who are used to chapters and verses, reading and studying the Bible without them may take a little getting used to. It's like when you get a new smart phone or move from using a laptop to a tablet. You have to unlearn some old ways of doing things and learn some new ways. But it's not too long until you catch on to how the new system works and you find you can do a lot of things you couldn't do before.

Here are some of the ways you and your group will have a better experience of the Scriptures by using these study guides.

YOU'LL FOLLOW THE NATURAL FLOW OF BIBLICAL BOOKS

This guide will take you through the book of Job following its natural flow. (The way the book unfolds is illustrated on page 9.) You won't go chapter-by-chapter through Job, because the chapter divisions in the Bible often come at the wrong places and break up the flow. Did you know that the chapter divisions used in most modern Bibles were added more than a thousand years after the biblical books were written? And that the verse numbers were added more than three centuries after that? If you grew up with the chapter-and-verse system, it may feel like part of the inspired Word of God. But it's not. Those little numbers aren't holy, and when you read and study Job without them, you'll hear its message more clearly than ever before.

To help you get a feel for where you are in the book's natural flow, sessions will be headed by a visual cue, like this:

Book of Job > Exchange of Speeches > First Round > Eliphaz

YOU'LL UNDERSTAND WHOLE BOOKS

Imagine going to a friend's house to watch a movie you've never seen before. After only a couple of scenes, your friend stops the film and says, "So, tell me what you think of it so far." When you give your best shot at a reply, based on the little you've seen, your friend says, "You know, there's a scene in another movie that always makes me think of this one." He switches to a different movie and before you know it, you're watching a scene from the middle of another film.

Who would ever try to watch a movie this way? Yet many study guides take this approach to the Bible. They have you read a few paragraphs from one book, then jump to a passage in another book. The UNDERSTANDING THE BOOKS OF THE BIBLE series doesn't do that. Instead, these study guides focus on understanding the message and meaning of one book.

Session 1 is an overview that will let you experience the book of Job as a whole. This will prepare you for considering its individual sections. Reading through an entire book at once will be like viewing a whole movie before zooming in on one scene. Groups that read books of the Bible aloud together have a great experience doing this. (If you've never done it before, give it a try—you'll be surprised at how well it flows and how fast the time passes.)

YOU'LL DECIDE FOR YOURSELVES WHAT TO DISCUSS

In each session of this study guide there are many options for discussion. While each session could be completed by a group in about an hour and a half, any one of the questions could lead to an involved conversation. There's no need to cut the conversation short to try to "get through it all." Group leaders can read through all the questions ahead of time and decide which one(s) to begin with, and what order to take them up in. If you do get into an involved discussion of one question, you can leave out some of the others, or you can extend the study over more than one meeting if you do want to cover all of them.

TOGETHER, YOU'LL TELL THE STORY

Each session gives suggestions for how the passage or passages you'll be discussing can be read in a way that brings out their form and meaning. In certain sessions you'll read out loud in parts like a play, and in other sessions you'll deliver the speeches that are given by the characters. This kind of telling and retelling of the biblical story is a spiritual discipline that allows people to take the Scriptures more deeply to heart. This discipline is very timely in a culture that increasingly appreciates the value and authority of story.

If you're using *The Books of the Bible*, you'll find that the natural sections it marks off by white space match up in most cases with the sections of the reading. If you're using another edition of the Bible, you'll be able to identify these sections easily because they'll be indicated in this guide by their opening lines or by some other means that makes them obvious.

EVERYBODY WILL PARTICIPATE

There's plenty of opportunity for everyone in the group to participate. Everyone can take turns reading the passages that you'll be considering. Group members can also read the session introduction aloud or the discussion questions. As a leader, you can easily involve quiet people by giving them these opportunities. And everyone will feel that they can speak up and answer the questions, because they're not looking for "right answers." Instead, they invite the group to work together to understand the Bible.

YOU'LL ALL SHARE DEEPLY

The discussion questions will invite you to share deeply about your ideas and experiences. The answers to these questions can't be found just by "looking them up." They require reflection on the meaning of each saying, in the wider context of the book it belongs to, in light of your personal experience. These aren't the kinds of abstract, academic questions that make the discussion feel like a test. Instead, they'll connect the Bible passage to your life in practical, personal, relational ways.

To create a climate of trust where this kind of deep sharing is encouraged, here are a couple of ground rules that your group should agree to at its first meeting:

Confidentiality. Group members agree to keep what is shared in the group strictly confidential. "What's said in the group stays in the group."

Respect. Group members will treat other members with respect at all times, even when disagreeing over ideas.

HOW TO LEAD GROUP STUDIES USING THIS GUIDE

Each session has three basic parts:

Introduction

Have a member of your group read the introduction to the session out loud to everyone. Then give group members the chance to ask questions about the introduction and offer their own thoughts and examples.

Reading

Have some read out loud the section of the book of Job that you'll be discussing. The study guide will offer suggestions for various ways you can do this for each session.

Discussion Questions

Most questions are introduced with some observations. These may give some background to the history and culture of the ancient world or explain where you are in the flow of the book. After these observations there are suggested discussion questions. Many of them have multiple parts that are really just different ways of getting at an issue.

You don't have to discuss the questions in the order they appear in the study guide. You can choose to spend your time exploring just one or two questions, and not do the others. Or you can have a shorter discussion of each question so that you do cover all of them. Before the meeting, group leaders should read the questions and the observations that introduce them and decide which ones they want to emphasize.

When you get to a given question, have someone read aloud the observations and the question. As you answer the question, interact with the observations (you can agree or disagree with them) in light of your reading from the Bible. Use only part of the question to get at the issue from one angle, or use all of the parts, as you choose.

(In some cases, reading and discussion will be combined, and discussion questions may also be asked in the introduction to a session.)

TIPS FOR HOME GROUPS, SUNDAY SCHOOL CLASSES, COMMUNITY BIBLE EXPERIENCES, AND INDIVIDUAL USE

If you're using this guide in a *home group*, you may want to begin each meeting (or at least some meetings) by having dinner together. You may also want to have a time of singing and prayer before or after the study.

If you're using this guide in a *Sunday school class*, you may want to have a time of singing and prayer before or after the study.

This study guide can also be used in connection with a *community Bible experience* of the book of Job. If you're using it in this way:

- Encourage people to read each session's Scripture passage by themselves early in the week. The exception will be session 1, when small groups or the whole church will gather to read or listen to the entire book or see it presented on stage. One recommended approach is to read through the book in small groups to begin with, in session 1, and then have a performance of it at the end of your community Bible experience, as a culmination of your time with the book and also as an outreach to your neighbors. You can offer an opportunity for questions and discussion afterwards.)
- Do each session in midweek small groups.
- Invite people to write/create some response to each small-group session that could be shared in worship that weekend. These might involve poetry, journal or blog entries, artwork, dramas,

videos, and so on, and especially the creative re-tellings that are invited in some sessions.

- During the weekend worship services, let people share these responses, and have preaching on the topic of the session that was studied that week. Speakers can gather up comments they've heard from people and draw on their own reflections to sum up the church's experience of that session.
- The following week will be devoted to the next session in the same way.

This guide can also be used for *individual study*. You can write out your responses to the questions in a notebook or journal. (However, we really encourage reading and studying the Bible in community!)

Note: Anytime you see *italicized* words in Scripture quotations in this book, the italics have been added for emphasis.

OUTLINE OF THE BOOK OF JOB

Numbers in parentheses indicate sessions in this guide.

Opening Narrative (2)

Job's Opening Speech (3)

Exchange of Speeches

First Round	Second Round	Third Round
Eliphaz (4) - Job (5)	Eliphaz - Job (10)	Eliphaz - Job (13)
Bildad (6) - Job (7)	Bildad - Job (11)	Bildad - Job (14)
Zophar (8) - Job (9)	Zophar - Job (12)	

The Hymn to Wisdom (15)

Job's Affidavit (16–17)

Elihu
First Speech (18)
Second Speech (19)
Third Speech (19)
Fourth Speech (20)

The LORD
First Speech (21)
Second Speech (22)

Closing Narrative (22)

EXPERIENCING THE BOOK OF JOB AS A WHOLE

Book of Job (Overview)

Before doing this session, have someone read aloud the material entitled "Why Read and Discuss the Book of Job?" at the beginning of this guide. Give everyone the chance to respond to this material and to talk about any previous experiences they've had with the book.

INTRODUCTION

It's not known exactly when and where the book of Job was composed. Many scholars believe that the cultural references it makes and the stage of the Hebrew language it employs point to a date around the fifth century BC, in Judea under Persian rule, although this cannot be established definitively. But the story itself is set in the land of Uz, which many interpreters locate in the Arabian desert to the east of Israel. This makes Job, the central character, one of the "people of the East," from the Israelite perspective of the book. Most commentators agree that the author began with an ancient account of Job, which may have been passed down from as far back as the time of Abraham (the earliest ancestor of the Hebrews). The author used this story at the beginning and ending of the book to provide a framework for the speeches. In other words, the book of Job is something like the historical novels we know today, which begin with actual people of the past and describe what they might have said and done at important times in their lives. The speeches in the book constitute a dynamic conversation between the contrasting but related ideas about God and humanity, suffering and blessing, that the people of Israel had formulated over the centuries in response to their own experiences of covenant relationship with God, of exile, and of restoration.

Behind the interplay of ideas in the exchange of speeches there's a basic plot that pulls the reader forward through the book. In the most basic terms, Job is the story of a traditional Hebrew *rib* or "covenant lawsuit." In ancient Israel, when two people had an agreement or understanding and one party felt that the other wasn't living up to it, this party would call for impartial referees (typically the community elders at the town gate) to hear their case, summon the other party to offer a defense, and then decide between them. Job feels that God isn't living up to his side of an implicit bargain: Fear me, do what's right, and all will go well with you. And so Job demands a hearing. His three friends Eliphaz, Bildad, and Zophar function roughly as the referees (although they're predisposed to believe that Job doesn't really have a case). But where is the defendant? Will God really appear to answer the charges, and if he does, can this contest between the Almighty and a mortal human being ever be settled fairly? These questions create an underlying suspense that culminates in a dramatic conclusion.

In this session you'll experience the book of Job as a whole, to prepare you to consider its individual sections in the sessions ahead.

READING

As a group, read the book of Job out loud together like a play, with people using their Bibles as scripts. (Job is found on pages 1197–1254 in *The Books of the Bible*. In other editions, you can find it in the Table of Contents.) This reading should take about an hour and a half. Have people take these parts:

Narrator
Job
Eliphaz
Bildad
Zophar
Hymn to Wisdom (explained in note 4, below)
Elihu
The Lord

NOTES

1. If you're using this guide in a small group, have your group members read the different parts. If you're using this guide for a community Bible experience, read through the book in small groups to begin with, then have a performance of it at the end of the experience, as a culmination of your time with the book and also as an outreach to your neighbors. Present it on a stage, if one is available. Encourage people who have acting experience to play the roles. You can offer an opportunity for questions and discussion afterwards. (As an alternative, you can gather your whole church, fellowship, or organization together for a read-through or dramatization of the book at the beginning of your experience with it, in session 1, without doing another presentation at the end.)

2. As you're listening to the book, you can follow how it unfolds by looking at the outline on page 9.

3. The narrator should read the story of Job at the beginning and ending of the book, as well as the brief introduction of Elihu that comes after the three friends stop answering Job. The other characters will recite their own speeches, but not read any parts they have within the opening and closing story.

4. A little over halfway through the book, there's an interlude in which a voice other than one of the regular characters speaks. This interlude is referred to by many interpreters as the Hymn to Wisdom. It comes right after Job answers Bildad's third speech (which is the last one any of the friends gives), and just before Job insists on his innocence and Elihu then speaks. (Note how, in the NIV, the quotation marks around Job's response to Bildad end just before this interlude, and how the book says after it, "Job continued his discourse.") It begins, "There is a mine for silver and a place where gold is refined," and it ends, "And he said to the human race, 'The fear of the Lord—that is wisdom, and to shun evil is understanding.'" (In traditional Bibles, the Hymn to Wisdom corresponds with chapter 28 of Job.) As we'll see in session 15, this interlude expresses the overall perspective of the book. Have a person other than the regular actors or narrator read this section.

5. This part of Job is by far the longest. It can be shared by a couple of readers if you wish. A good place to switch would be right after the Hymn to Wisdom.

6. As an alternative to reading the book out loud yourselves, you can listen together to a professional recording. If you do, you should find one that uses the NIV, since that's the version used in *The Books of the Bible* and in this study guide. The *NIV Audio Bible* by Zondervan is available through Christian bookstores and many online outlets. You can also visit www.biblegateway.com to listen to the book of Job from the NIV for free. However, your group will probably have the best experience doing your own reading and acting.

DISCUSSION

After the reading, discuss the following questions. (If you're using this guide in a community Bible experience, you can either divide into smaller groups or stay all together for a larger discussion.)

⟳ Had you ever seen a book of the Bible presented as a play or read in parts like this? If so, tell the group briefly about that experience. How was encountering the book of Job in this way different from other ways you may have read it or other biblical books? Did this give you any new ideas about what the Bible is? Explain.

⟳ What parts of the book are you most looking forward to discussing in more detail in the sessions ahead? Why?

⟳ If you could ask the author of Job one question about this work, what would you ask?

⟳ At the end of the book, Job finally gets his hearing, but after God states his own case, Job says he won't reply, even though he's given the opportunity. Based on this initial encounter with the book, do you find this ending satisfying? Why or why not?

THE ADVERSARY DESTROYS JOB'S POSSESSIONS, FAMILY, AND HEALTH

Book of Job > Opening Narrative

INTRODUCTION

As you saw last time, the book of Job begins with a narrative (story) that sets the stage for the speeches that follow. The story introduces the character of Job and then describes how he met with a series of terrible misfortunes.

Several of the other characters in this story require some explanation for modern readers:

- The LORD (Hebrew *Yahweh*) is the name God used when he made his covenant or special agreement with the people of Israel. The book of Job is set outside of Israel in patriarchal times (that is, in the days of Abraham, Isaac, and Jacob), so in the speeches God is called by other names, such as *Shaddai* ("the Almighty"), *Qadosh* ("the Holy One"), and *Eloah* (an ancient word for God). But the book is written for a Jewish audience, and the author wants them to know that this is their God, the Supreme God, Creator of the world, so in the framework story God is called the LORD.

- The "angels" (literally "sons of God") are agents who patrol the earth and report back to God about what they observe.

The ancient Hebrews envisioned a "heavenly council" that was convened to deliberate important matters (it's described as the "great assembly" in Psalm 82). This council is portrayed here. Persian emperors had special officials who roamed secretly throughout their empire in ordinary clothes and reported back to them about exemplary citizens worthy of promotion and troublemakers to be dealt with. If the book was indeed written in the Persian period, these officials may have provided some of the coloring for this opening story.

• In this story, "Satan" is not actually a name. The Hebrew word *satan* literally means "adversary," and in the book of Job it's always preceded by "the," so this is actually a title: "the Adversary." The word *satan* is used many times in the First Testament to describe a determined and persistent opponent, as in the account of Solomon's reign in Samuel–Kings: "Rezon son of Eliada . . . gathered a band of men around him and became their leader . . . Rezon was Israel's *adversary* as long as Solomon lived . . . Rezon ruled in Aram and was hostile toward Israel." As a noun, the root *satan* is used in a specialized way to describe an accuser in a legal proceeding; as a verb, it describes the act of accusing, as in Psalm 38: "My enemies . . . *lodge accusations* against me." Here in the book of Job, the Adversary is both a determined opponent of God and an accuser of anyone who seeks to follow God faithfully. This character is much like the devil or Satan described in the New Testament, although the portrait isn't drawn as fully here in the book of Job. The book doesn't account for where he came from or how he became opposed to God, but it does portray him as a crafty and malicious player within the complex moral web of the universe.

READING

Read the opening narrative of the book of Job out loud like a play. Have people take these parts:

Narrator

Job

The LORD

Satan (the Adversary)

First messenger

Second messenger

Third messenger

Fourth messenger

Job's wife

(In the dialogues between the LORD and Satan, the narrator doesn't need to read cues like "Satan answered . . . Then the LORD said," etc.)

As you read this narrative together, note and appreciate the ancient setting it re-creates, where a person's wealth is measured in livestock and servants, and the head of a household functions as its priest. Also note how it often repeats phrases (for example, "fears God and shuns evil," "I am the only one who has escaped," etc.) to create a rhythmic solemnity in its storytelling even as the events rush forward to a catastrophic outcome. There's an elegance and symmetry to the language in this narrative that expresses respect for the importance of its subject. (For example, the same Hebrew root meaning "fall" is used in the phrases "the Sabeans *attacked*," "the fire of God *fell*," "the house . . . *collapsed*," and "Job . . . *fell* to the ground in worship.")

DISCUSSION

1 Like the "sons of God," the Adversary has been roaming around the earth. But his goal hasn't been to advance the LORD's purposes; rather, he's been looking for any opportunity to undermine them. The LORD asks whether he's seen Job, who is living testimony to the benefits of fearing God and shunning evil. The Adversary knows all about him (for example, that "his flocks and herds are spread throughout the land"), and he's ready with an insidious accusation: Job is only loyal to God *because* he's being blessed. "Strike everything he has," he insists, "and he will surely curse you to your face."

The book of Job has much to say about the *problem of evil*, that is, why there is so much suffering in the world if it's governed by a good God. As we consider the book in detail in the sessions ahead, we'll get many insights into this question. But here the Adversary begins by raising a different problem, the *problem of good*. If apparent goodness is always rewarded and bad conduct is always punished, how can we ever really be sure that a person is genuinely good and not just trying to win rewards and avoid punishment? It turns out that the only kind of universe in which genuine good can be known to exist is one in which good people sometimes suffer undeservedly but still demonstrate continuing loyalty to God.

On the level of ideas, the book is already challenging the view about rewards and punishments that prevailed in its day. And on the level of the plot, the Adversary has sprung a trap that requires the LORD to allow him to torment Job and try to get this exemplary servant to curse God. Or has he? Perhaps the LORD has sprung the trap instead. The Adversary will only embarrass and discredit himself in the end, if Job's goodness and loyalty are proven to be genuine.

⮎ One of the most disturbing thoughts for readers of the book of Job is the idea that the devil could somehow trick God into allowing him to harm a loyal person of faith. But the interaction here is much more complex than that simple interpretation implies. The Adversary can only believe that Job is motivated by greed; the LORD knows that Job's heart is actually pure and devoted. And so the LORD permits, or perhaps even arranges, a test in which the devil's worst efforts actually disclose the truth about Job's good heart, and about the possibility of goodness generally. If, through suffering without knowing why, you could help demonstrate for an audience on earth and in heaven that cynical, disparaging, diabolical contradictions of God's ways are false and unfounded, would you be willing to do this?

⊃ The glimpse we get here at the beginning of the book into the heavenly council isn't designed to give us a right answer to carry with us all through the intricate debate that follows. In other words, this story isn't intended to make the simple case that whenever a good person suffers undeservedly, this is a test designed to demonstrate that genuine goodness can exist. Rather, given the lengthy and complex moral reflections that follow, we should see this as *one possible explanation*—presumably among many—for why a good person might suffer. The strategic goal here is to show that, even on its own terms, a belief in inevitable rewards for goodness is fatally weakened by an internal difficulty. This clears the ground for a free exchange of alternative ideas in the speeches that follow. What other possible reasons can you suggest for why a good person might suffer undeservedly?

2 Job, unfortunately, knows nothing of the role he's intended to play in vindicating God's ways, so when his sufferings come, they're not tempered by any sense of purpose or meaning. The Adversary makes these horrible misfortunes sting as cruelly as possible. He takes away Job's possessions and then, when his only comfort is the thought that at least he still has his family, the Adversary takes away his children as well. (Job's blessings are stripped away in the reverse order of their original mention: He loses first his oxen and donkeys, then his sheep and camels, and finally his sons and daughters.) The Adversary does all of this in rapid succession on the eldest son's birthday, a milestone day that Job was always aware of, as the story shows. Ultimately Job is stricken with a skin disease ("painful sores") that requires him, for hygienic and ceremonial reasons, to leave his community and sit "among the ashes"—in the garbage heap outside the settlement. There a shard of broken pottery becomes his only possession, a crude tool to scrape off some of the worst effects of his sores. From the way the Adversary goes about doing what God gave him permission to do, it appears that he's trying to get Job to believe that his sufferings aren't random, they're personal—that at the heart of the universe, there's a hostile, malevolent presence that's out to get him.

⮑ Have you ever suffered, for reasons you didn't understand, in a way that stung cruelly? (For example, was a special occasion or a significant birthday or anniversary ruined by an experience that will always be a bad memory, or was a treasured possession accidentally and senselessly destroyed?) Did this suffering convey a message about the nature of the universe that you've believed, consciously or unconsciously, ever since? In light of Job's experience as it's related here, is it possible that the sting behind your suffering came from God's Adversary, who wants you to believe that God is hostile and uncaring? Can you talk back to yourself about these beliefs and free your mind from the effects of this diabolical message?

3 Job's wife is a much-maligned character in this story. She appears to side with the Adversary by wanting Job to curse God. But as usual in this book, there's much more going on here than appears on the surface.

As we'll note frequently in the sessions ahead, the book of Job presents many contrasts, tensions, paradoxes, ironies, and surprises. As the story opens, there is coherence between Job's beliefs and his experiences. He fears God and shuns evil, he believes that this course in life leads to blessing, and he's being blessed. But Job's experiences have now come into sharp tension with his beliefs. His life seems to demonstrate instead that his beliefs and practices do not lead to the ends he expects, but he continues in them anyway. His wife is advocating for a restored coherence between his beliefs and his experiences. There seems to be no way to change the experiences themselves—not if God is as hostile as he appears—and so the solution is to adopt a new kind of belief and practice. "God obviously wants to be your enemy," Job's wife is saying (and she has suffered and lost just as much as he has), "so why don't you just admit it, and become his enemy, too?" This is a logical and reasonable response to everything that has happened. The only alternative is to abandon the belief that a devout course of life inevitably leads to earthly blessings but to still maintain the belief that one should be loyal to God anyway, for reasons to be determined. Within the book, the purpose of the challenge Job's wife offers is to push both him and the reader into this alternative.

The God whom Job's wife wants him to curse is not the same God Job chooses to keep trusting in. She wants him to curse a God who supposedly blesses goodness but who can capriciously turn against a loyal servant. He decides to continue trusting in a God who is more complex, more unfathomable, and more perplexing than he may previously have thought but who is in the end far truer to experience and more genuinely deserving of praise and worship.

⮑ Answer the following question on your own behalf or on behalf of someone you know: Have you ever lost the coherence between what your beliefs led you to expect of God and what you were experiencing in life? Did this loss of coherence lead you to "curse" (reject) the God you then believed in? Did this ultimately lead to a renewed loyalty to a more unfathomable but more trustworthy God? If so, tell the group what happened.

⮑ Whose side would you say Job's wife is ultimately on? What leads you to that conclusion?
   a. The LORD
   b. The Adversary
   c. Neither one, exactly.
   d. Both, in some ways.

⮑ Job responds to his initial misfortunes by describing the LORD as one who both gives and takes away. He answers his wife's challenge by saying that if we accept good things as from God, then we need to accept troubles in the same way. Have you ever had an experience where you were able to accept God taking something away from you, or where you were able to accept troubles as something God might have a purpose in, because you recognized that you also accepted good things from God? If so, share your experience with the group.

⭮ Conclude your time together, if you wish, by singing Matt Redman's song "Blessed Be Your Name," which is based on Job's words in this story.

JOB WISHES HE'D NEVER BEEN BORN

Book of Job > Job's Opening Speech

INTRODUCTION

Job and his friends sit together in silence for a week. Then, in one of the surprises that will come to characterize the book, Job suddenly breaks the stillness with an anguished cry for death to release him from his torments. He wishes, in fact, not just that he could die, but that he had never lived. The abrupt shift from what seemed like a serene acceptance of his fate to a loud and bitter protest against it is another of the vivid contrasts that keep this book alive with tension and energy. This is the first of the long series of speeches in the book that will explore the most fundamental questions of human existence.

READING

Have someone read Job's opening speech out loud for the group. (Like all the speeches in the book, its limits are clearly indicated within the text, as each of the speakers is announced in turn.)

As you listen, notice that the speech has three main parts:
> Job curses the day he was born.
> Job wishes for rest in the grave.
> Job asks why people who no longer want to live aren't allowed to die.

DISCUSSION

1 In the first part of his speech, Job wishes that the day of his birth and the night of his conception had never existed, because if they hadn't, he would never have come into existence himself. His grief and anguish are so great that he no longer believes life is worth living.

In this part of the speech, Job calls for an un-creation. The image of darkness obliterating light is used repeatedly. This reverses the creation account in Genesis, where God first brings order out of chaos by saying, "Let there be light!" Job says literally of his birthday, "That day—let it be darkness!" In a sense the night has a light of its own; not just the moon and stars, but an inherent light as part of the ordered creation that was brought out of primordial darkness. So Job asks for darkness to obscure the night as well, for the "morning stars" (or "twilight stars") to go dark.

Job calls on those who are "ready to rouse Leviathan" to use their powers to curse the day of his birth. Leviathan is a sea-monster who represents the forces of chaos. Job wants this chaos monster to un-create the day he was born, so it will no longer be "included among the days of the year." Job's formerly stable and prosperous life suggested that he lived in a harmonious universe where God's rule was uncontested. But now he describes a very different world, in which the forces of order and chaos are locked in unending battle and where, at times, people may actually be better served by chaos.

When the LORD answers Job at the end of the book, he will also speak of light and darkness, and of Leviathan, to reveal a very different picture of the creation. But this is still a long way off. At this point, Job's life is so shattered he wishes it had never even begun.

⮑ In the opening story, Job's sons observe their birthdays with great feasting and celebration. But now Job doesn't want his birthday to be observed at all; he doesn't even want it on the calendar. This is because he now considers his existence worthless and pointless. Is there a day each year that you wish wouldn't come? If so, what day, and why? How has what happened on this day made you feel about the purpose and significance of life? (Once again you can answer either for yourself or for someone you know.) While honoring the genuine loss and sorrow of those who feel this way about certain days, how would you encourage them to think differently about their lives? (Caution: This is not an easy question to answer, as Job's friends will soon discover.)

2 In the next part of the speech, Job speaks longingly of the grave as a place where he could be "lying down in peace . . . asleep and at rest." He describes it as a universal resting place for small and great alike. "Kings," "rulers," and "princes" are there, no matter how much wealth and power they once had.* Captives and slaves are freed from their harsh labor, and the wicked no longer cause any trouble.

Job is describing how, from an earthly perspective, death is the great equalizer, humbling the powerful and granting relief to the oppressed. Once again the idyllic picture of the book's opening, in which Job's servants lived peacefully and prosperously with him and his family, is displaced by a different description of life on earth, in which slave drivers shout at their captives while rulers heap up treasures. This inequality and oppression will be ended in the grave and, Job says wistfully, so will his own trials.

⮑ Should people who are experiencing suffering or oppression find consolation in the thought that these things will be ended when they die? Are there some conditions that will never be remedied on this earth? Or can people who are concerned for justice be hopeful that any given expression of injustice or oppression might be overcome in this life?

⮑ If we can't take our treasures with us and any monuments we build will one day lie in ruins, what things are worth living for?

---

* These same three terms are used, in this order, to describe officials of the Persian empire twice in the biblical book of Ezra. This is one of several suggestions in the book of Job that it was written during the Persian period. Another is the description of caravan trade that you'll encounter in session 5; this trade was fostered by the Persians.

3 In the final part of the speech, through what is actually one long, elaborate question, Job asks why "light" (meaning "life," but echoing the opening image of the speech) is given to those who "long for death." Job describes people, including himself, who "search for [death] more than for hidden treasure." This anticipates the central image of the Hymn to Wisdom, in which the search for wisdom is compared to the search for treasures hidden in the earth. But Job is searching for death, not wisdom, indicating that he has given up on finding any meaning or purpose in his life. He just wants it to be over.

Job describes himself as a person "whom God has hedged in." This is the exact language the Adversary used when he said that the LORD had "put a hedge around" him. But the usage here is ironic. Job means something very different by this phrase—not that God has protected and preserved him, but that God has surrounded him with inescapable trouble and misery.

⟳ Have you ever had a friend or loved one pass away after a long, lingering illness that kept them in constant pain and robbed them of all enjoyment in life, so that you were actually relieved for them when they died? Would you say that, for some people, a time does come when life is no longer worth living? Has that time come for Job at this point in his life?

ELIPHAZ URGES JOB TO TRUST GOD

Book of Job > Exchange of Speeches > First Round > Eliphaz

INTRODUCTION

Job's three friends have come to "sympathize with him and comfort him." So when he breaks his silence and despairingly wishes for death, they try to respond with words of encouragement and hope. Over three rounds of speeches, they reply to various arguments that Job makes.

The first to speak is Eliphaz the Temanite. Teman was a region in the country of Edom that was renowned for its wisdom. (The prophet Jeremiah once asked, for example, "Is there no longer wisdom in Teman? Has counsel perished from the prudent?") Because Eliphaz speaks first and has the most to say, he is likely the most senior of the friends in age, learning, and reputation.

Eliphaz reminds Job of the conventional understanding of life in the wisdom tradition of the ancient world. He explains that the wicked may flourish briefly, but God will always make sure they don't harm or oppress the innocent for long. ("The lions may roar and growl, yet the teeth of the great lions are broken." "I myself have seen a fool taking root, but suddenly his house was cursed.") God can be relied on to punish the wicked and reward the righteous, so Job should turn to him in this time of trouble.

READING

Have someone read Eliphaz's first speech out loud for the group.

As you listen, notice that the speech has these main parts:

Opening words of encouragement to Job.

General summary of wisdom teaching: The innocent are protected but the wicked perish.

Report of a night vision.

Destruction of the wicked.

Trustworthiness of God.

Protection of the righteous.

DISCUSSION

1 "If I were you," Eliphaz tells Job, "I would appeal to God; I would lay my cause before him." Job indeed wants to lay his cause before God; as he'll say shortly, he wants the chance to appear before God and argue that he's done nothing wrong, so God must have been wrong to afflict him. But Eliphaz has something very different in mind. The implications of his speech are that Job must have been secretly doing something wicked that led to his downfall, so he should confess and forsake whatever this was and expect that God will then restore his fortunes. (Eliphaz subtly echoes the symbolism of Job's opening speech to place him among the wicked: "Darkness comes upon them in the daytime," he insists, "at noon they grope as in the night," alluding to Job's wish that the day of his birth would "turn to darkness.")

Eliphaz's speech echoes the themes of the book of Proverbs and the wisdom psalms.* It's an eloquent expression of the wisdom teaching found generally in the Bible. And yet, even at this stage in the book, the reader knows that Eliphaz is somehow wrong. At the end of the book, the LORD will actually say that Eliphaz has "not spoken the truth about me." How can this be?

---

* You can find out more about Proverbs and the wisdom psalms in the guides in this series to biblical wisdom literature (*Proverbs/Ecclesiastes/James*) and lyric poetry (*Psalms/Lamentations/Song of Songs*).

The problem is that Eliphaz is treating a general truth as if it were a universal one, and so in his mouth it's becoming a mistruth. Everything he says is generally the case: God does protect the innocent from the oppression of the wicked, even if the wicked do flourish briefly. But it's not the case that every single time a person suffers misfortune, God must be punishing them for wickedness. Eliphaz would have done well to listen to his own wisdom teaching and recognize that God's wonders ultimately "cannot be fathomed." Mortal human beings must always leave ample space within their theological systems and life philosophies for God to work in unexpected, inexplicable, and even perplexing ways, and they must still give God the benefit of the doubt.

⮑ What other examples can you give of life principles that are generally true, but not necessarily universally true? Describe special cases in which an appeal to these principles could be a misdiagnosis and a mistruth.

⮑ Eliphaz's speech illustrates the general human tendency to look first for someone to blame when things go wrong. Blaming God for causing Job's sufferings unfairly would shatter Eliphaz's elaborately articulated view of the world, so he can only blame Job. How about you: Can you live in a world in which awful things sometimes happen but there's really no one to blame?

2 Knowing that Eliphaz's speech describes an understanding of the world that's generally true, even if not universally true, helps us appreciate and engage it as an articulate expression of that understanding.

⮑ Eliphaz says, "Hardship does not spring from the soil, nor does trouble sprout from the ground. Yet man is born to trouble as surely as sparks fly upward." He doesn't just mean that human life is inevitably filled with troubles; he's saying that most of the troubles in the world are caused by people, not by natural forces. Do you agree? Why or why not?

⊃ In the classic wisdom style, Eliphaz tells the innocent, "From six calamities [God] will rescue you; in seven no harm will touch you." He then enumerates seven kinds of trouble. (The meaning of these diverse Hebrew terms is not entirely understood; the NIV translates two of them as "famine" and two others as "destruction," along with battle, "the lash of the tongue," and wild animals.) Can you describe a time when you believe God rescued you from a calamity like one of these? What danger were you in? What makes you believe that God in particular rescued you? Can this be a meaningful and reassuring experience for you even if faithful people aren't always rescued in this way?

⊃ Eliphaz promises the innocent that they will have a "covenant with the stones of the field." In a vivid metaphor, he suggests that the stones will actually agree to stay out of cultivated areas, so that fields will be easy to till and become very productive. Do you believe it's generally true that when people are living right, God creates conditions that will make them prosperous? Explain why you agree or disagree.

⊃ What do you appreciate most about Eliphaz's speech as a statement of general truth? What parts of it ring true to your experience and view of the world, even if there may be specific exceptions?

3 Visions like the one Eliphaz describes in this speech may have earned him a reputation as a seer, that is, someone who got occasional glimpses into the unseen world that helped him understand the basic principles of life.

⊃ What is your reaction when you hear someone describe a vision that's supposedly from God or from an angel or spirit that God has sent?

    a. I'm interested in what this person has to say, because I think this is an important way God speaks to us.

   b. I'm open-minded and willing to listen, but I maintain a
     healthy degree of skepticism.

   c. I stay as far away from this kind of thing as possible.

Why do you respond like this?

JOB ASKS HIS FRIENDS TO UNDERSTAND AND SYMPATHIZE

Book of Job > Exchange of Speeches > First Round > Job's Response to Eliphaz

INTRODUCTION

Eliphaz finishes speaking and gives Job a chance to respond. In his reply, Job could dispute whether Eliphaz's argument really applies to him—he could say yes, God does punish the wicked, but I'm not wicked, so something different must be happening in my case. Or he could question Eliphaz's entire premise and insist that rewards and punishments in this life don't necessarily correspond with innocence or guilt. He will do both of these things in his later speeches, but in this one he responds on a relational level. Job appeals to his friends to understand why he has spoken so bitterly and despairingly. It's not because he's wicked or no longer trusts God. It's because he's in such physical and emotional agony. What he needs most from them is sympathy and understanding, not an analysis of why he's suffering.

In the second half of the speech, Job speaks directly to God, once again on a relational level. He asks God to recognize how brief his life on earth is. Does God really want him to spend most of it suffering for his sins? Why not ease up on him, forgive him, and let him enjoy a few moments of life without God as his constant enemy?

READING

Have someone read aloud Job's response to Eliphaz's first speech. This person should address the group in the opening part of the speech, and then speak as if to God from the point when Job asks, "Do not mortals have hard service on earth?"

DISCUSSION

1 Job begins by explaining that his words have been "impetuous" because he's suffering so greatly. He uses the image of contented eating as a contrasting illustration: "Does a wild donkey bray when it has grass, or an ox bellow when it has fodder?" Of course not. And he's only been braying and bellowing because he's in anguish. Job then speaks literally of eating to describe one of the effects of his physical suffering: Food no longer tastes good to him; he's too distressed to eat. During the rest of his speech he graphically describes his other mental and physical sufferings, including both sleeplessness and nightmares, and the effects of his skin disease. But he returns to the image of eating and tasting as he finishes addressing his friends. He asks, "Is there any wickedness on my lips? Can my mouth not discern malice?" In other words, even if I can't taste my food anymore, I would still "taste" and recognize wrong speech if it was in my mouth. So even though I've been speaking this way, please believe in my innocence and integrity. Don't take my emotional, even rash words as a sign that I have abandoned my trust in God.

⮑ Is what people say in moments of pain and desperation an accurate expression of what they truly think and feel inside? That is, do extreme circumstances strip away all pretense and posing, so that a person's core convictions are exposed? Or should we not hold people entirely responsible for what they say at such times, on the premise that their pain is making them say things they don't really mean?

⮑ In what ways might it help a person to let them speak out of their pain, and in what ways would it be helpful to encourage them to be extra careful about what they say when in pain?

2 The centerpiece of the first part of this speech is an extended image in which Job describes his friends as "intermittent streams." They are like *wadis* that travelers count on for water when crossing the desert, but which "stop flowing in the dry season," so that caravans have to "turn aside from their routes" to search for water. They "go off into the wasteland," the trackless part of the desert, but they find nothing and ultimately perish. Based on how his friends treated him when things were going well, Job expected them to be an abundant source of refreshment when they came to encourage him in his trials. But they have "proved to be of no help." They've left him dying of thirst.

Job explains that he's not really asking that much of them. They don't need to pay an expensive ransom for him or fight with him against his enemies. He just needs them to look him in the eye and believe in him. But they are afraid—perhaps afraid that if they associate too closely with him, God will strike them too.

⮑ If you've gone through a major trial in your life, were there people who helped you by simply being there for you and believing in you? How do you think they were able to recognize that this was what you needed from them?

⮑ Job says, "Anyone who withholds kindness from a friend forsakes the fear of the Almighty." In other words, if you abandon a friend in their time of need, you're not someone who truly honors and obeys God. Do you agree? What kinds of things might keep a well-meaning person from coming alongside a friend who's in trouble?

3 When Job addresses God, he first describes human life as something that seems to pass slowly because of its misery and futility. But he then describes how it actually passes very quickly. Humans are here today and gone tomorrow—and permanently gone, since "one who goes down to the grave does not return. He will never come to his house again." (Job is describing things from an earthly perspective. Even though he will later express confidence in an afterlife, he is appreciating the earth as a place where people have one limited opportunity to relate to God in a unique way.)

Given the brevity of human life, Job wonders why God seems to be such a stern disciplinarian. It's not as if Job is one of the primal elements of chaos ("the sea, or the monster of the deep"—like Leviathan in session 3) that God needs to keep closely under guard so it won't destroy the creation. Echoing the language of Psalm 8, but in an ironic sense, Job asks, "What is mankind that you make so much of them, that you give them so much attention, that you examine them every morning and test them every moment?" He ultimately asks God, "If I have sinned, what have I done to you? . . . Why do you not pardon my offenses and forgive my sins?" In other words, since we're really so insignificant, why don't you just cut us some slack and enjoy a good relationship with us here on earth while you can?

⮑ Do you think of God as a stern disciplinarian who constantly watches people and punishes them for the slightest infractions? (Job is speaking to God here as if Eliphaz were right about him, as a way of *replying to Eliphaz*, but as readers of the book we are invited to make our own judgments about this view.) If you don't think such a portrayal of God is accurate, where would you say people get this idea?

⮑ How would you answer Job's question here: When we sin, does this do something to God? Does it require God to respond in some way?

⮑ Can God deal with sin by pardoning and forgiving it, as Job suggests here? Do you think God might do this for the sake of having a good relationship with people while they're alive on earth?

BILDAD URGES JOB TO "PLEAD WITH THE ALMIGHTY" TO ESCAPE THE FATE OF THE WICKED

Book of Job > Exchange of Speeches > First Round > Bildad

INTRODUCTION

The next friend to address Job is Bildad the Shuhite. (Many interpreters locate Shuah, his home region, in the area of Mesopotamia, meaning that Job's friends have come some distance from both the east and the west to speak with him.)

Bildad's speech follows the same general outline as Eliphaz's. It begins with some words addressed directly to Job; it then commends the ancient wisdom teachings; and finally it describes the destruction of the wicked and God's blessings on the righteous. But while Eliphaz spoke cautiously and diplomatically, Bildad takes the gloves off. He accuses and confronts Job right from the start.

READING

Have someone read Bildad's first speech out loud for the group. As you listen, notice how it follows the pattern described above.

DISCUSSION

1 Bildad accosts Job as if he were a prosecuting attorney trying to browbeat a suspect into taking a plea bargain. He insists that all of Job's children died because God "gave them over to the penalty of their sin." But since Job himself is still alive, he must not have sinned quite so badly. There is still hope for him. If he will "seek God earnestly and plead with the Almighty," confessing his sin and asking for forgiveness, God will restore his "prosperous state." In fact, Bildad promises, "Your beginnings will seem humble, so prosperous will your future be."

Bildad is encouraging Job to act just like the person the Adversary said he was: someone who doesn't "fear God for nothing," but who is good for the sake of the blessings and riches he expects to get in return.

⊃ Have you ever heard someone promise material prosperity as a reward for following God? Describe briefly who this was and what they said. Would you agree that following God's ways does lead a person to make wiser choices and be more disciplined, so that eventually they do become better off financially? If this is a likely *result* of following God, how can it be prevented from becoming a *motive* for following God?

2 Bildad was listening carefully to Job's response to Eliphaz. He picks up on Job's observation about the brevity of life and suggests that a different conclusion can be drawn from it. Job wanted to encourage God not to be so severe with people that they never have a chance to enjoy a peaceful relationship with him during their short time on earth. But Bildad says the implications of life's brevity are that people should trust in the wisdom of experience accumulated over many generations: "Ask the former generation and find out what their ancestors learned, for we were born only yesterday and know nothing, and our days on earth are but a shadow." According to Bildad, the ancient wisdom teaches that sufferings are punishment for sin, so Job, based on his own words, should stop insisting on his own innocence. Like Eliphaz, Bildad is misapplying a general truth by treating it as a universal truth. He can't recognize that Job's situation is an exception. But we can still engage his appreciation for the wisdom of the ages as something that's generally appropriate.

⤳ Which does your culture value and encourage more: learning and following traditional teachings or developing creative original ideas? What are the dangers when a culture emphasizes one of these so much that the other is ignored or suppressed? Which would you like to do more in the years ahead: learn about traditional ways and understandings or explore innovative ideas and approaches? Why?

3 Bildad also picks up on Job's reference to a water plant ("Is there flavor in the sap of the mallow?") to develop a series of natural metaphors, beginning with papyrus and then continuing on to spider webs and garden plants. Bildad reveals a keen eye for detail, describing, for example, how roots wind around rocks. But his observations all have hidden barbs. The wisdom tradition customarily balanced descriptions of the destruction of the wicked with depictions of the prosperity of the righteous. But Bildad's metaphors, which make up the largest part of his speech, are all about how the godless perish, so they're all aimed at Job. He is like the formerly thriving reed that has now withered; his confidence has given way like a spider web; he's been uprooted from his place. Only a few brief lines at the end of the speech promise restored joy and pleasure if Job will distance himself from evildoers.

Even though Bildad is once again wrong about Job's particular situation, he's demonstrating a breadth of learning. As the friends speak, they reveal how they have become renowned for their wisdom. Eliphaz has built his reputation as a seer; Bildad has done so as a naturalist.

⤳ What have you seen in the natural world that has illustrated some aspect of human life for you? What popular sayings do you know that teach lessons through natural metaphors? (For example, "The early bird gets the worm," "Every cloud has a silver lining," etc.) Do you believe that people who study the natural world can learn things there that help them understand God's ways and human experience better?

JOB WISHES HE COULD TAKE GOD TO COURT

INTRODUCTION

Bildad encouraged Job to "plead with the Almighty," meaning that he should beg him for mercy. But Job picks up on this idea and considers how he might plead in a different sense: by entering into a legal "dispute" with God. (The term is *rîb*; it describes a traditional Hebrew covenant lawsuit. Job uses the term again when he asks God what "charges" he has against him.) Job feels that God has violated an understanding and agreement they had. God was supposed to punish the guilty and bless the innocent, but Job is being punished even though he's innocent, as far as he's concerned. If only there were some way to meet God on equal terms, before an impartial arbitrator, and settle things!

In this response to Bildad, Job reflects on this idea and the inevitable difficulties surrounding it. Once more he speaks first to his friends and then addresses God directly.

READING

Have someone read aloud Job's reply to Bildad's first speech. As in session 5, the reader should address the group in the opening part of the speech, and then speak as if to God from the point where Job says, "I say to God: Do not declare me guilty."

DISCUSSION

1 Job would really like to take God to court, but he realizes the difficulties are insurmountable.

First, God is a being of infinite power. Job knows he needs someone who can "mediate between us" and "bring us together," literally "lay a hand on us both," that is, put us both under the authority of the law. (The friends are not providing this kind of impartial mediation.) Then, Job says, he would "speak up without fear" of God. But as things stand now, he's afraid that God will use his infinitely superior power to crush any protest. In fact, Job accuses him of being arbitrary and indifferent: "He destroys both the blameless and the wicked." At the beginning of this speech, Job describes God's power and greatness. He even echoes a line directly from Eliphaz's speech ("He performs wonders that cannot be fathomed, miracles that cannot be counted"). But while Eliphaz wanted to depict God as trustworthy, Job uses the same kind of language ironically, to suggest that God can't be trusted to be fair, since he can enforce his will on anyone. He even "treads on the waves of the sea . . . The cohorts of Rahab [another name for the chaos monster] cowered at his feet."

A second difficulty is that God is also a being of infinite wisdom. God can always recognize something that Job could have done differently or better, and he can detect motives that Job isn't even aware of that taint his best-intentioned actions. So there's no way for Job to prove that he's innocent in any sense that God would accept. So Job is concerned that if he did try to bring God to court, he would not "give me a hearing." Rather, "he would crush me with a storm." Since God does come to Job in a "storm" (the same Hebrew term is used) at the end of the book, this prediction creates some suspense as the storm gathers and approaches.

⊃ Followers of Jesus often talk about having a "personal relationship with God" through their faith in him. But what kind of relationship can finite beings actually have with a being whose power and wisdom are infinite, since they are infinitesimally small by comparison? What assurances do we have that God isn't using his greater knowledge and power to manipulate this relationship to his own advantage, without us knowing it or being able to do anything about it? (To help answer this question, suppose you make a new friend who has a four-year-old child. You want to be genuine friends with this child as well. How would you relate equitably with him or her, despite your advantages of power and knowledge?)

⊃ The New Testament describes Jesus as a "mediator between God and mankind." Do you think that Jesus is a mediator in the sense that Job describes here—someone who wants to help resolve any outstanding dispute between God and humans and who is equally sympathetic to both parties?

2 When Job turns to address God directly, he asks him about something that doesn't make sense to him: "Does it please you to oppress me, to spurn the work of your hands?" In other words, why would God lovingly and carefully craft Job into such an intricate being ("your hands shaped me and made me"), only to watch him constantly afterwards with suspicion and hostility, ready to pounce on any wrong move? Job uses vivid metaphors from the world of crafts to describe God's creativity in making him: Milk being curdled into cheese represents how God gave form to his body; sewing and knitting depict how he was "clothed" with flesh and bones. Wouldn't a craftsperson, Job wonders, take delight in their creation, rather than regard it with hostility? Job acknowledges that he has experienced God's kindness and watchful care in the past, but his recent misfortunes make him think that God was harboring mistrust all along.

⊃ What features and capabilities of your own being and personality lead you to see yourself as an intricate creation of

God? What expressions of God's kindness and care have you experienced that lead you to believe he treasures you as one of his fine artistic achievements? If God is an artist in this way, is it consistent for him to watch people suspiciously to catch them in anything they might do wrong? Or would God's aesthetic pleasure in people as his creations make him more likely to pardon and forgive them, as Job wishes he would?

3 At the end of this speech, Job says that if life on earth really is spent under the glaring eye of an arbitrary and hostile God, then it's actually better never to be born. He reprises the darkness imagery of his opening speech to describe the abode of the dead, where he wishes he had gone straight from birth, as "the land of gloom and utter darkness." (There may be a hint of this same conclusion earlier in the speech, when Job describes God's power by saying, "He speaks to the sun and it does not shine; he seals off the light of the stars.")

⮑ Is life really not worth living if God is arbitrary and hostile, and only annihilation follows death? If we have a stubborn innate sense that somehow life is worth living, can we conclude from it that the picture of God presented in this speech must not be accurate?

ZOPHAR APPEALS TO THE HIDDEN SIDE OF WISDOM

Book of Job > Exchange of Speeches > First Round > Zophar

INTRODUCTION

The friends are taking turns responding to Job, so the last of them, Zophar the Naamathite, now speaks. (The location of his home region is uncertain, although some interpreters believe it was to the northwest of the land of Israel. Once again this would be some distance from Job's home in Uz, in yet another direction.) Many interpreters conclude that Zophar is the least senior of the friends, since he speaks last, most briefly, and only twice instead of three times like the others.

Zophar's speech incorporates some of the same basic elements as the other friends' speeches. He begins by addressing Job directly. Then, like Eliphaz, he extols the greatness of God. Finally, like the other two friends, he describes the destruction of the wicked and God's blessings on the righteous. But in this part of the speech his tactic is opposite to Bildad's. He talks almost entirely about what the righteous can expect from God, with only a brief mention of the wicked at the end.

READING

Have someone read Zophar's first speech out loud for the group. Notice how it includes the elements described above.

DISCUSSION

1 Like the other friends, Zophar has been listening carefully to Job. He, too, picks up on his language and imagery and interacts with it. Job has asked, in reply to Eliphaz, why God can't just pardon any sins he may have committed, so he can spend his few days on earth in peace. Zophar tells him that "true wisdom has two sides," meaning an open side, evident to general human view, and a secret side, known to God and perhaps, in part, to those who search after wisdom. One hidden truth that Job hasn't yet grasped, Zophar insists, is that God has already granted his wish and forgotten some of his sin. In other words, while Bildad suggested that Job was spared his children's fate because he was less wicked, Zophar insists that both Job and his children deserved to be killed, but that God has shown him mercy in the hopes that he will "put away [his] sin."

Job knows this isn't true, and readers of the book know this as well from the opening story. Zophar has misapplied his insight into the "two sides" of wisdom because of his inflexible view of the world: He thinks all suffering must be punishment for sin. But we can still engage this insight as one that potentially discloses one of the "secrets of wisdom."

⮑ Do you think that there are "two sides" to knowledge or wisdom, an open side accessible to observation, investigation, and rational analysis, and a hidden side that's only partially accessible to people, through means such as philosophical and theological reflection and divine revelation? Or do you believe that all truth and knowledge is ultimately accessible to empirical investigation?

⮑ If you do believe there are two sides to wisdom, how do the means of investigating these sides relate to one another?

a. Are they two different ways of confirming the same truths?

b. Is each one a separate means of understanding distinct truths that are not accessible to the other?

c. Or is there some overlap between their domains, so that some truths can be known by one, some by the other, and some by both?

➲ We see from Job's friends what damage can be done when a partial understanding of the hidden side of wisdom is held inflexibly as if it were comprehensive. What can a person do to remain humble, flexible, and generous as they speak about the insights they believe they've gotten into the hidden side of wisdom?

2 Zophar responds directly to something else that Job has said. In his reply to Bildad, Job demanded a legal hearing where he could make God answer charges. Zophar responds, "I wish that God would speak." He's confident that if Job actually did get this hearing, God would immediately show him he was in the wrong. Zophar praises God's infinite power and wisdom and concludes, "If he comes along and confines you in prison and convenes a court, who can oppose him?"

This was precisely Job's question in the previous speech. Job wanted to know what assurance people could have that God wasn't using his advantages of power and wisdom unfairly—a profound and disturbing question that might possibly be answered, at least somewhat, after much reflection. For Zophar, the implications of this question ("Who can oppose God?") are entirely different. He simply concludes that people must accept whatever God does without question. If there's anyone to blame, they should blame themselves.

Zophar doesn't realize that this conclusion is inconsistent with his own argument. If God's ways truly are unfathomable, as he describes, then people like himself can't know with certainty and confidence what God is doing. Zophar is actually putting the authority of God's infinite wisdom and power behind his own *interpretation* of what God is doing in Job's case. This, simply stated, is spiritual abuse.

⮑ Abuse in general is using some form of violence or coercion to take away another person's dignity and freedom. This can be done through angry outbursts, degrading language, confinement, physical or sexual assault, and so forth. Another type of abuse is spiritual: People are told that if they don't conform their actions and beliefs to particular expectations, they are wicked and evil, and an all-knowing, all-powerful God will punish them. Have you ever witnessed or experienced spiritual abuse like this? What effect does it have on how a person sees and relates to God? How can a person learn to recognize spiritual abuse, refuse to put up with it, and recover from its effects?

3 In his concluding words about how God blesses the righteous, Zophar continues to take up Job's earlier language and imagery and employ it for his own purposes. Job had wished for the day of his birth to become darkness; Zophar tells him, "Life will be brighter than noonday, and darkness will become like morning." Job had wished for rest in the grave; Zophar promises, "You will . . . take your rest in safety." Job had complained to God, "When I think my bed will comfort me . . . even then you frighten me with dreams." Zophar counters, "You will lie down, with no one to make you afraid."

Mockingly throwing another person's words back in their face is not constructive or respectful. But that's not necessarily what Job's friends are doing in cases like this. Rather, when they echo words and images that Job has used, it's more likely that they're trying to explore with him whether these might have other meanings and implications that he could consider. These implications might lead him to moderate or alter his views. (Job himself picks up on their language in this same way, as we've noted.) Ultimately the friends have a simplistic and inflexible view of the world that will not hold up under this kind of sophisticated interplay of ideas. But they are modeling a potentially powerful and profitable way to engage differences of understanding.

⮑ What examples can you give of recent debates or discussions you've heard in which opposing sides suggested different meanings for the same key terms and images? Did the debaters do this in a constructive way, shedding greater light on the range of meaning and application that these terms and images could have? Or did they do it destructively, trying to shut down all meanings but their own and belittling or attacking those who held different views?

⮑ Identify a belief or approach you don't agree with. How could you respond to it by drawing out different meanings and implications from the language that's characteristically used to defend it? Do you find that this is a method you can use constructively to promote discussion and encourage people to explore wider ranges of understanding? Or do you feel that some of the people you'd like to engage this way are, like Job's friends, too inflexible for this approach to work with them? What makes people inflexible like this?

JOB INSISTS HE'S AS WISE AS HIS FRIENDS AND AGAIN ASKS GOD FOR A HEARING

Book of Job > Exchange of Speeches > First Round > Job's Response to Zophar

INTRODUCTION

Job's reply to Zophar is the longest so far. In fact, it's the longest speech he gives in the entire book except for his affidavit at the end of the exchange of speeches with the friends. This speech is so long because it's a summary response to what they've said in the whole first round. Once again Job starts by addressing them, and he then turns to address God.

As he speaks to the friends, Job first seeks to demonstrate that he has just as much wisdom and knowledge as they do. At the beginning and end of this demonstration, he insists, "I am not inferior to you." Job then tells the friends he has no confidence in them to "speak . . . on God's behalf." They've been functioning effectively like community elders at a city gate, giving him a preliminary hearing to determine whether he has a valid case to bring before God, like a grand jury today. (And in this guise, they've actually been trying to convince him he doesn't have a case.) Job announces he has no confidence in their integrity or impartiality, and so, he says, the best thing for them to do is keep silent and let him deal directly with God.

Job then addresses God and proposes terms for a hearing. If God will agree not to strike or intimidate him, God can choose whether he'd like to be the plaintiff or the defendant: "Summon me and I will answer," Job says, "or let me speak, and you reply to me." Without waiting for an answer (he doesn't really expect one), Job assumes the part of the plaintiff and interrogates God, as he did in his two previous responses to the friends.

READING

Have someone read aloud Job's reply to Zophar's first speech. Once again, the reader should address the group in the opening part of the speech, and then speak as if to God from the point where Job says, "Only grant me these two things, God . . ."

DISCUSSION

1 Job demonstrates to the friends that he's not inferior to them in wisdom or knowledge by mimicking at length their conventional way of speaking about God and the world. He shows that he has full command of the language and ideas in their repertoire. But midway through this extended demonstration, he gives the standard presentation a twist and depicts God not as someone who predictably punishes the wicked and blesses the righteous, but as someone who unexpectedly and inexplicably brings disaster on everyone—great and small, wise and foolish alike. Zophar had insisted that God "surely . . . recognizes deceivers." Job counters that "both deceived and deceiver are his," that is, they are in his power: God might destroy the innocent as well as the guilty.

The wisdom tradition celebrated God as creator, suggesting that he had built the way of wisdom into the very fabric of the world. Proverbs, for example, says that God "gave the sea its boundary so the waters would not overstep his command"—he tamed the watery forces of chaos to create habitable space. But here Job depicts God as an un-creator. He "holds back the waters" so there is drought or "lets them loose" so they devastate the land. The biblical creation account, as we noted earlier, begins with God bringing light out of darkness. But Job says instead that God "brings utter darkness into the light." His understanding of how God's power is displayed in the natural world encompasses disturbing observations and questions that the friends won't even entertain. While this makes Job's understanding less comfortable, it's also more sophisticated and realistic.

⊃ Do you think disasters on earth could have a number of different explanations? In the friends' view, they are always punishments. But what if only some disasters were punishments, while others were intended as corrections, and still others had an unidentifiable purpose? If disasters had these different possible explanations, would this make you feel you could trust God more, or would it make you trust him less?

⊃ Job tells the three friends that they're acting as if wisdom will "die with you." In other words, they seem to believe that the wisdom of the ages has reached its culmination in their generation and that they understand things comprehensively. This is despite their own warning to Job that individual people's lives are so short that even the community of godly people only comes to understand things cumulatively over a great deal of time. So they should believe instead that they are somewhere *on the way* to greater wisdom. Have you been encouraged to hold certain beliefs about God and the world as if they were comprehensive and definitive? Which of these beliefs might you hold more provisionally, if greater insight may be coming in the future? Which understandings do you think are unlikely to be improved upon by later generations?

2 Even though the friends are upholding the pious party line of their day, Job accuses them of speaking "wickedly" and "deceitfully" on God's behalf. What he means is that they're fabricating evidence. In their view, God predictably rewards the innocent and punishes the guilty; it seems that Job is being punished; therefore, he must be guilty of something. Without any real evidence of what this might be, they've been telling him that he has plowed evil and sown trouble and is now reaping it; that he needs to "put away the sin that is in [his] hand"; and so forth. Job warns them that if God examined their evidence (actually, their lack of it), things would not turn out well for them, so the best thing they can do is stay silent.

⮑ When things happen that seem to call God's goodness and love into question, do you tend to "fill in the blanks" and supply certain facts not in evidence in order to make the situation fit a more comfortable picture of God? If you've done this about a current situation, try withdrawing your supplied explanations and saying instead, "I don't know exactly why this happened, but God doesn't need me to make things up to help him look better." How does it feel to approach the situation this way?

3 When Job turns to address God, he takes up some of the same themes he explored in his previous responses to the friends. For example, he once more describes the brevity of human life and asks why God doesn't "look away" from people and leave them alone, since they are insignificant, transient creatures who can't be affecting him that much. But this speech also represents an important advance on the previous ones, as Job begins to make connections between his various reflections. Job again wishes for rest in the grave, where, he believes, he will be safe from the anger God is now directing against him for reasons he can't understand. But he also envisions a time in the future when God will no longer be angry with him and will seek him out, even in the grave, since (as he also suggested earlier) God will "long for the creature [his] hands have made."

In other words, for the first time in the book, Job may be talking about an afterlife. But if he is, in order to show that he doesn't mean he would ever live on this earth again, he draws a contrast between a tree sprouting again after being cut down and people staying in the grave. Nevertheless, somewhere, at some time, with his anger past, God will remember him and call for him, and he will answer.

⮑ The time after a person's death is often regarded as a time when God's disposition towards them becomes permanently fixed, either positively or negatively. But Job suggests here that while God seems to be negatively disposed toward him at present, in the future, some time after his death, God will become positively disposed instead. Where would this idea fit, if at all, within your present understanding of what happens to people when they die? Why do you think this suggestion is offered here in the Bible? If you do think that God might "long for" a departed person who was not in his presence after their death, on what basis would God be positively drawn towards them? How might God "call" to them?

JOB LOOKS FOR SOMEONE TO BELIEVE IN HIM

Book of Job > Exchange of Speeches > Second Round > Eliphaz
Book of Job > Exchange of Speeches > Second Round > Job's Response to Eliphaz

INTRODUCTION

Even though Job has urged his friends to keep silent, they continue trying to convince him that he must have done something wrong to deserve his suffering. In one of the book's great ironies, while these friends have supposedly come to "sympathize with him and comfort him," Job finds that they are instead "miserable comforters." But their challenges do lead him, in his responses, to keep reflecting deeply about his situation and to gain further perspectives on it.

The friends once again take turns speaking, in the same order, with Eliphaz going first. In this second round their speeches and Job's replies are shorter, so we will now consider both parts of each exchange in a single session.

READING AND DISCUSSION

1 Have someone read Eliphaz's second speech out loud for the group. As you listen, notice that it has these main parts:

Opening words of accusation against Job.

Praise of the ancestors' teaching.

Description of the destruction of the wicked.

Like Bildad in his first speech, Eliphaz in this second speech praises the traditional teaching that has been passed down from the ancestors. He believes it supports their claim that Job's sufferings must be the result of his sins. To encourage Job to respect this tradition and become humble and penitent, Eliphaz challenges him with a series of questions: "Are you the first man ever born? Were you brought forth before the hills?" And so forth. This technique, known as a "wisdom interrogation," is used often in the book of Job, and at particular length here. The LORD will use it more extensively and artfully than any previous speaker when he addresses Job at the end of the book.

Once he has finished his questioning, Eliphaz once again expounds the implications of the ancestors' teaching, as he understands it. But instead of depicting both the destruction of the wicked and the prosperity of the righteous, as all the friends did to some extent in the first round, he only describes, at length, how the wicked are destroyed. Eliphaz thinks that he and his friends have so far been speaking "gently" to Job, but since he isn't getting the message, they need to threaten and terrify him so he will admit his guilt and beg for mercy.

⮕ Have you ever heard a speaker encourage people to turn to God primarily by describing the destruction that awaits them if they don't? What picture of God does this leave people with? What motive does it give them for following God? (What would the Adversary say about this motive?) What is the proper place for this kind of description within an overall presentation of the challenge and opportunity of following God?

⮕ Eliphaz says that his teaching has been passed down from the time when there were "no foreigners" in the land of the ancestors. If the book is actually addressing a Jewish audience in the Persian period, this would correspond with the time before the exile when Israel was politically and culturally independent. For such an audience, Eliphaz would represent the position that Jews will become corrupted if they absorb too many ideas from the other cultures they've become exposed to. Within the book itself, Eliphaz is making a subtle suggestion that Job has been getting too many of the wrong ideas from the wrong places. How have you been encouraged to relate to learning and ideas that do not explicitly reflect your own religious tradition? Have you been told that since "all truth is God's truth," you can learn valid things from other channels of inquiry? Or have you been warned against exposure to "worldly" ideas that will corrupt you? What opportunities and dangers do secular studies and the ideas of other religious and philosophical traditions present for followers of Jesus?

2 Have someone read Job's reply to Eliphaz. Note that, as in his previous replies, Job speaks first to the friends (in this case, quite briefly) and then directs the rest of his remarks to God. But in this case he alternates back and forth between talking *to* God and talking *about* him.

In his response to Eliphaz's second speech, Job describes how greatly he is suffering, just as he did in response to Eliphaz's first speech. But this time he doesn't talk about his sleeplessness, loss of appetite, nightmares, and skin disease—his physical symptoms. Instead, he describes the social aspects of his suffering: how people are mocking and accusing and abandoning him because of his physical condition, which they consider a "witness" against him that he is guilty. But even though people on earth are reaching this conclusion, Job insists that he has another witness in heaven, someone who can see the truth about him and who will testify on his behalf if he can get God to hear his case. Job doesn't identify who this "witness" or "advocate" or "intercessor" is. He just seems to be confident, for some reason, that among the heavenly beings there is at least one who will recognize that he's being unfairly accused and speak up for him.

⮑ Who are the "mockers" who surround you? That is, what people in your life, and what voices echoing in your head, unfairly accuse you of being and doing the wrong things? Followers of

Jesus today consider him to be their advocate and intercessor in heaven. How would Jesus, who knows you truly, testify on your behalf against these voices and set the record straight about your best motives and intentions?

3 Job says, "Give me, O God, the pledge you demand. Who else will put up security for me?" The pledge or security that Job is describing is the ancient equivalent of bail. An accused person, or a friend on their behalf, would surrender a valuable possession as a guarantee that if set free, the accused would show good conduct and appear in court. Job wants to be freed from his relentless suffering so he can properly organize and present his case.

Everyone on earth believes he is guilty, so none of them will put up security for him. But Job still has somewhere to turn. Even though his case is against God, he's so convinced that God knows he's innocent that he paradoxically asks God himself to provide this pledge. This shows that, beneath all of his questions and accusations, Job still maintains a degree of trust and confidence in God. (It also suggests that the "witness" Job has in mind may be God himself.)

⊃ Do you call on God to help you even at times when it seems as if he's out to get you? If so, where do you get the confidence to ask God for help when this seems so contrary to your circumstances? If this is hard for you to do, what helps you in those times? (How do you think Job developed a confidence that survived all of the disasters he experienced?)

ACCUSED BY HIS FRIENDS, JOB DECLARES THAT GOD WILL BE HIS REDEEMER

Book of Job > Exchange of Speeches > Second Round > Bildad

Book of Job > Exchange of Speeches > Second Round > Job's Response to Bildad

INTRODUCTION

At the end of his response to Eliphaz's second speech, Job urged the friends to "try again" to help him, before death took him and there was no more hope. So now Bildad speaks again. But he only repeats, with even greater insistence, the friends' belief that Job must be suffering because of his own guilt.

In response, Job describes his sufferings once more. He notes, as he did in reply to Eliphaz's second speech, that his greatest pain comes from being rejected and abandoned by his family and friends. But this ultimately leads Job to make an even bolder and more daring declaration: Though everyone else has forsaken him, in the end God himself will come and vindicate him.

READING AND DISCUSSION

1 Have someone read Bildad's second speech out loud for the group.

The friends' earlier speeches contained a variety of elements, including praise to God as the just ruler of the world, depictions of how the righteous are blessed, and encouragement to Job about his future. But in this speech, after addressing Job only briefly, Bildad talks exclusively about how the wicked will be destroyed. While this is a standard component of general wisdom teaching, Bildad makes it personal. He changes from an impartial grand juror into a prosecuting attorney as he weaves the facts of Job's specific situation into his presentation to demonstrate that Job is among the wicked.

Bildad says of the wicked man, for example, "Calamity is hungry for him . . . It eats away parts of his skin." This is a direct reference to Job's skin disease, which is horrifying and disfiguring, and which everyone is taking as proof of his guilt. Bildad is implying that Job has been given a death sentence and is already experiencing the effects of death—decomposition—while he is still alive. Bildad also says that the wicked man "has no offspring or descendants among his people." Since all of Job's children have been killed, this must be further evidence against him. And Bildad asserts, "Terrors startle him on every side," alluding to the way Job said God was "terrifying" him. At the beginning and end of his speech, Bildad describes the wicked person by using the imagery of light and darkness: "The light in his tent becomes dark"; "He is driven from light into the realm of darkness." This recalls Job's opening speech, in which he wished the day of his birth had been darkness and not light. In all of these ways, Bildad uses Job's own words to condemn him. Job had accused the friends of fabricating evidence of his guilt; Bildad feels the evidence is plain for all to see. It has come from Job's own mouth.

⮑ You're a single young woman and you meet a young man at your church. As you chat with him, you discover that he's not working or in school but rather has been "looking for work," as he puts it. He also has a black eye for some reason. As you're saying goodbye to one another in the parking lot, you notice that his car has two large dents in it. Just then he asks you out on a date. Do you believe you have enough evidence to conclude that you should turn him down? Or do you decide that none of these things you've noticed are actually his fault, it's just a coincidence that they've all happened at once, and he's the kind of young man you'd like to pursue a relationship with?

2 Have someone read Job's response to Bildad's second speech. As you listen, notice that it has these main parts:

Job addresses the friends directly.

He describes how God has attacked him.

He says that all of his relatives and acquaintances have abandoned him.

He expresses his confidence that God will vindicate him in the end.

He warns the friends not to keep accusing him.

Job acknowledges that his body is wasting away. "I am nothing but skin and bones," he admits. His foul-smelling and disfigured body is making everyone he knows avoid him. But he insists that it's not actually death that has been consuming him alive; it's the pitiless accusations of his supposed friends. He asks, "Will you never get enough of my flesh?" Job's worst suffering is not physical; it's relational. By unjustly accusing him instead of supporting him, his friends are doing far worse to him than his skin disease ever could.

⮑ If you had to choose between (1) experiencing great physical loss and suffering, but having a strong community of family and friends to support you, or (2) remaining healthy and prosperous, but having everyone who's close to you unfairly believe that you've done wrong and abandon you, which would you choose? Why?

⮑ What person who's presently in a time of great loss or suffering can you come alongside and encourage, even if you can't do anything to change their situation?

3 Once again Job paradoxically finds hope in God, even though God also appears to be afflicting him without cause. His earthly relatives and friends have all abandoned him, but he remains confident that God will be his "redeemer." This term (*goel* in Hebrew) refers to a person in ancient Israel who ensured that a needy family member or friend had someone to advocate for them, defend them, and provide for them. This role goes beyond that of serving as a legal witness. It implies identification with another person's interests and a commitment to see them restored to a secure situation in life.

The text here is difficult to translate and interpret. Job may be saying that his skin disease will not prove fatal before God comes in person to vindicate him. "After my skin has been destroyed," that is, despite the effects of this disease, "yet in my flesh" (while I am still alive) "I will see God." "In the end," as my case is finally resolved, "he will stand upon the earth." In other words, Job is not, as Bildad suggested, a dead man walking, just about to fall into the grave. He is undergoing horrible afflictions, but they will not be the end of him. Job has an astonishing confidence that the very same God who has caused or allowed his present suffering will ultimately come to his rescue.

Job's words can also be understood as an expression of faith in the afterlife, and specifically in the resurrection of the body. Many interpreters hold that "after my skin has been destroyed" means "after I die," and that "in my flesh I will see God" means "in a resurrected body." They understand the phrase "in the end he will stand on the earth" to refer to God appearing, and specifically to Jesus returning, at the end of human history.

But it's not ultimately necessary to try to decide between these interpretations. The first one suits the overall plot of the book, in which God indeed appears on earth "in the end," declares that Job has spoken rightly of him while the friends haven't, and restores Job to his former state. The second interpretation suits the immediate context, in which Job is concerned that he will die before he is vindicated and so wishes for his words to be recorded on a scroll or engraved on a rock so that his case can be resolved even after he is gone. Whether Job is paradoxically expecting God to vindicate him in this life or after his death, either possibility would be consistent with much of what he has already said.

⊃ Has a friend or relative ever acted as a redeemer for you at a time when your resources weren't sufficient for your own situation? If so, tell the group briefly about this. Have you ever been this kind of redeemer for someone else?

⊃ What do you think Job, who's deathly ill, destitute, and abandoned, expects God to do about his situation as his redeemer? What further reflections do you have about how Job was able to develop this kind of enduring hope in God, despite everything that happened to him?

⊃ Does this explanation of the role of a *goel* help you understand better what the New Testament means when it describes Jesus as our redeemer? What would it look like for him to be your redeemer in a practical or spiritual way right now?

ZOPHAR ACCUSES JOB OF BECOMING RICH BY OPPRESSING THE POOR

Book of Job > Exchange of Speeches > Second Round > Zophar
Book of Job > Exchange of Speeches > Second Round > Job's Response to Zophar

INTRODUCTION

In this second round of speeches, Eliphaz and Bildad have concentrated on describing the destruction of the wicked in order to convince Job to admit his guilt and beg for mercy. Zophar has been listening carefully to the evidence they've offered. He has reached a conclusion about what Job's specific sin must be. He insists, in a long discourse on the destruction of the wicked, that Job must have acquired his wealth by oppressing the poor. This is why all that wealth was taken from him in an instant: This was a punishment that fit the crime.

Job does not defend himself against this specific accusation here, although he will do so later in the book. Instead, he breaks completely with the friends' main premise and offers an extended rebuttal of the idea that good deeds are rewarded and bad deeds are punished consistently here on earth. Earlier he expressed some qualified agreement with this idea ("Who does not know all these things?"), but now the friends have driven him to the point where he must insist it isn't true to broad human experience and so it doesn't provide a comprehensive explanation of why people prosper or suffer.

READING AND DISCUSSION

1 Have someone read Zophar's second speech out loud for the group.

Like the other friends' speeches in this round, Zophar's is devoted almost entirely to describing how the wicked are inevitably destroyed, even if they prosper briefly. Like Bildad, Zophar tailors this supposedly general description to fit Job's specific situation. He uses the image of tasting and eating as an extended metaphor to depict how the guilty pleasures of the wicked suddenly abandon them: They lose their appetites and nauseously spit out the riches they've gobbled down. This is a pointed reference to the way Job said earlier that food had become tasteless to him. Zophar also describes how God's arrows strike the wicked and pierce their internal organs, recalling how Job said, "He has made me his target; his archers surround me. Without pity, he pierces my kidneys and spills my gall on the ground." Zophar also uses the images of terrors and darkness against Job, as Bildad did. But he makes his sharpest attack when he challenges Job's confidence that witnesses will ultimately come forward to vindicate him. In the Hebrew culture, heaven and earth were traditionally called upon as symbolic witnesses, since they were ever present and all-seeing. So Job had earlier cried, "Earth, do not cover my blood," and insisted, in an ingenious twist on the usual formula, not that heaven was his witness, but that he had a witness in heaven. But Zophar declares instead, "The heavens will expose his guilt; the earth will rise up against him." These two primal witnesses will testify against Job, not for him.

Zophar says all of this is to assert, like the other friends, that Job's sufferings and his own descriptions of them are proof that he is being punished for some wrongdoing. But Zophar goes beyond the other friends' claims to accuse Job of a specific crime: heaping up wealth for himself by oppressing the poor. Zophar believes there's no way Job could have become so fabulously wealthy if he were really playing by the rules. "He has oppressed the poor and left them destitute," Zophar insists. "He has seized houses he did not build." But now he adds, "Nothing is left . . . Such is the fate God allots the wicked."

⮑ Google Inc. acknowledges that it is a business, and a profitable one, but one of the main points of its corporate philosophy is, "You can make money without doing evil." Do you agree? Or do you think a person or a company can only make so much money without doing evil, but beyond this, if they're accumulating huge amounts of wealth, they must be doing something wrong?

2 Have someone read Job's response to Zophar's second speech. Notice that in this speech, Job no longer directs himself to God at any point. He just challenges the case the friends have been trying to make.

After listening to three speeches about how the wicked are destroyed, Job has heard enough. He answers them all with the assertion that actually the wicked are not destroyed. They may live their days out in prosperity and security, and go peacefully to their graves.

This is likely what Job has believed all along. If he really shared the friends' view, he would have been asking them from the start to help him figure out what he'd done wrong so he could become prosperous again. The friends have provoked him into expressing himself quite starkly, but this is his core belief: Rewards and punishments on this earth don't correlate consistently with how people live. (This belief is closer to the perspective of Ecclesiastes than to the general outlook in the book of Proverbs, but it's still within the broad stream of wisdom teaching in the Bible.)

What Job says here actually provides a definitive refutation of the Adversary's claim that he served God because he thought this would make him prosperous. It turns out that Job never did believe this. He says it terrifies him to admit it, but his observations of life actually lead him to conclude that the wicked are more likely to prosper than the righteous. Even so, he chooses not to live as they do: "I stand aloof from the plans of the wicked." So Job in fact served God even though he believed that faithful people, in general, don't do as well in this life as the wicked.

⮑ If you're a follower of Jesus, do you believe that this is likely to cost you something in this life? In other words, will there be opportunities, experiences, relationships, and material advantages you will not be able to enjoy if you want to follow Jesus faithfully? What might some of these things be specifically? Why would you say it's still worth it to follow Jesus?

⮑ The friends have been accusing Job unfairly because they've been regarding a general truth as if it were comprehensive. Job now replies to them as if his general observations about the prosperity of the wicked were comprehensively true. ("Their bulls never fail to breed," etc.) Have they provoked him into overstating his case? Do you think that, within the wider community of Jesus' followers today, innovative thinkers are sometimes pushed towards more extreme conclusions than they would otherwise reach? If so, how does this happen?

⮑ Zophar insists that he's describing "how it has been from of old." Job counters, "Have you never questioned those who travel? Have you paid no regard to their accounts?" Once again the debate pits Job's more cosmopolitan perspective against the friends' stubborn loyalty to the beliefs passed down from their ancestors. What's the most significant way in which a travel experience has helped you understand something new about life and God?

⮑ Job anticipates an objection the friends will offer to his argument: Even if the wicked themselves aren't punished, their children will be. He counters that if a person is genuinely wicked, they won't care what happens to their children. It's only the righteous who are concerned with giving their children a secure and prosperous future. Let God "repay the wicked," he insists, "so that they themselves will experience it!" Would you feel that some justice had been done if a wicked person escaped conviction and punishment during their lifetime but afterwards their family didn't get to keep the profits from their crimes?

ELIPHAZ RENEWS THE CHARGE THAT JOB HAS OPPRESSED THE POOR

Book of Job > Exchange of Speeches > Third Round > Eliphaz

Book of Job > Exchange of Speeches > Third Round > Job's Response to Eliphaz

INTRODUCTION

Each of three friends has now spoken twice, but they still haven't succeeded in persuading Job of their view that he must be suffering because he has done something wrong. So they give it one last try, beginning again with Eliphaz.

In his third speech, Eliphaz doesn't address what Job has just said in reply to Zophar, that the wicked generally prosper and go unpunished in this life. Rather, Eliphaz joins Zophar in accusing Job of a particular sin: oppressing the poor in order to become rich. While Zophar spoke generally of "the wicked," Eliphaz accuses Job personally and charges him with specific offenses, for example, "You gave no water to the weary and you withheld food from the hungry."

In response, Job doesn't defend himself directly against these charges (although he will do so a little later in the book, as we've already noted). Instead, he characteristically picks up on the ideas and images in Eliphaz's speech and uses them to continue making his own case: He is not among the wicked, and if he could only get a hearing before God, he would be vindicated.

READING AND DISCUSSION

1 Have someone read Eliphaz's third speech out loud for the group. As you listen, notice that it has these main parts:

Eliphaz questions Job's goodness in an opening "wisdom interrogation" (a series of challenging questions).

Eliphaz levels specific charges against Job.

Eliphaz encourages Job not to think that God is so distant and hidden that he can't see what he's doing and hold him accountable.

Eliphaz urges Job to abandon the wicked pursuit of riches so he can be forgiven and restored.

In his reply to Eliphaz's first speech (session 5), Job suggested that human sin doesn't affect God so much that he must always be on the lookout for it and punish it: "If I have sinned, what have I done to you, you who sees everything we do?" But here in his third speech, Eliphaz suggests the opposite, that human *goodness* has no effect on God: "What pleasure would it give the Almighty if you were righteous? What would he gain if your ways were blameless?" Eliphaz concludes that no matter what good things Job may have done, they have no offsetting value; God must still punish him for every one of his sins.

➲ Which claim about God have you heard more often: that God puts no value on human goodness and is focused on identifying and punishing sin; or that God can forgive or overlook human sin without doing any damage to his own character and authority? Within the context of the book of Job, should we be more inclined to accept the second claim, because Job makes it, rather than the first claim, since Eliphaz makes it?

➲ Does it make God happy when people are good?

2 Have someone read Job's response to Eliphaz's third speech. Notice that it has these main parts:

> Job wishes he could state his case before God.
>
> Job complains that he can't find God—he's too elusive.
>
> Job describes how the poor and needy are oppressed and wishes God would rescue them.
>
> Job describes how the wicked try to hide but will ultimately be punished.

As he characteristically does in response to the friends' speeches, Job takes Eliphaz's own words and images and reemploys them. For example, Eliphaz insisted that God can see people through the "darkness" and "clouds" that separate him in the heavens from them on earth. Job agrees with this. He describes in his own speech how evildoers try to hide in darkness, thinking, "No eye will see me," and how God discovers and punishes them just the same. But Job also counters that for his part, he can't see God through the "thick darkness" that stands between them. This is why he hasn't been able to track God down and arrange for a hearing that would vindicate him. Eliphaz also used the image of precious metals to insist that Job should treasure God rather than riches ("Assign your nuggets to the dust . . . Then the Almighty will be your gold, the choicest silver for you"). Job picks up on this language when he says that after God has tested him, "I will come forth as gold." This, Job insists, is what he truly treasures: his integrity as a person who fears God and shuns evil.

⮑ As Job explains here, human beings can't meet with God in person to defend their conduct and find out why certain things have happened to them. Job doesn't know yet that in his exceptional case, God will come to speak with him directly. Nevertheless, he expects that somehow, as a result of his present trials, it will become clear that he has "kept to [God's] way without turning aside." How do you think he expects this to happen? By what means today can the true motives behind a person's conduct become apparent? How can people reach a better understanding of the troubling events in their lives and see them more from

God's perspective, even if they're not able to meet personally with God to discuss this?

3 In these speeches both Eliphaz and Job give many specific examples of how the poor and needy are oppressed by the wicked. After giving his own examples, Job seems to take back some of what he said in reply to Zophar's second speech, that the wicked generally prosper. Instead, he describes how God punishes and destroys the wicked. One possibility is that Job now realizes that he overstated his case in response to Zophar, and he is correcting himself. Alternatively, Job may be expressing his wishes ("May their portion of the land be cursed," etc.) rather than describing general conditions. The Hebrew verb forms allow for either possibility. In the second case, Job would be saying that even though the wicked appear to be getting away with their oppression, his fervent wish is that God would stop them and punish them. This is the same position he took in his reply to Zophar when he said, "I stand aloof from the plans of the wicked." (Eliphaz ironically echoes this phrase in his third speech, to imply that Job is among the wicked!)

⊃ As a group, look again at the second part of Eliphaz's speech and the third part of Job's response and identify all the specific ways in which they depict the poor and needy being oppressed by the wicked. In Eliphaz's speech these will be accusations against Job, for example, "You gave no water to the weary." In Job's speech, they will be descriptions of the wicked ("There are those who move boundary stones") or of the sufferings of the oppressed ("They have nothing to cover themselves in the cold"). Explain in each case what the depiction means within the ancient culture in which the book of Job was written. Then describe what an equivalent would be today. What specific things have you seen followers of Jesus do to help people in some of the situations of oppression and need that are described here? What could your group do about one of these specific situations?

⊃ Have you ever heard about someone doing something so wicked and oppressive that it made you wish God would punish them? If so, describe briefly for the group what this was. Is there a place for followers of Jesus to feel this way and to express these feelings to God in prayer, even though their general mission is to proclaim God's forgiveness and mercy?

THE FRIENDS FINISH SPEAKING WITH JOB

Book of Job > Exchange of Speeches > Third Round > Bildad
Book of Job > Exchange of Speeches > Third Round > Job's Response to Bildad

INTRODUCTION

The end of the third round of speeches presents several elements that are unexpected and puzzling. Bildad gives only a very short third speech, and Zophar gives none at all. This departure from the pattern established in the first two rounds is actually the kind of surprise that the book of Job loves to spring on its readers. It also vividly creates the impression that the friends are running short of things to say, and then running out entirely, as their argument fails to persuade Job. However, despite these positive features of the present arrangement, because of the content of the speeches themselves, most interpreters believe that the text here at the end of the third round has become somewhat disordered.

Bildad's brief speech praises the power and greatness of God. This theme is then developed further in Job's reply, just after his opening rebuke of the friends. Many interpreters believe that this material was originally part of Bildad's speech and that it was accidentally transposed into Job's reply at some point. They suggest that another part of Job's reply, the last section, which describes the fate of the wicked, was also originally spoken by one of the friends. Job at least wished for the punishment of the wicked in his reply to Eliphaz's third speech, but the tone here is so smug and pedantic ("I will teach you about the power of God") that many interpreters believe this material may originally have been part of a third speech by Zophar, which has now been mostly lost.

It's not possible to know for certain whether there has actually been a disturbance in the text here. But in this session we will follow the broad consensus of interpreters and treat some parts of Job's reply to Bildad as if they belonged to speeches originally given by the friends.

READING

Have someone read Bildad's third speech and the part of Job's reply that begins, "The dead are in deep anguish, those beneath the waters and all that live in them," and ends, "Who then can understand the thunder of his power?" (This part of Job's reply begins just a few lines after the text says, "Then Job replied" [to Bildad].)

Then have someone read Job's reply, beginning at the start but skipping over the part that has just been read with Bildad's speech, resuming where it says, "And Job continued his discourse," and ending with "May my enemy be like the wicked, my adversary like the unjust!" (Again, these are relatively short pieces of Job's speech.)

Finally, have someone read the rest of Job's reply, beginning with "For what hope have the godless when they are cut off, when God takes away their life?" and ending with "It claps its hands in derision and hisses him out of his place."

DISCUSSION

1 If Bildad's third speech once included the material in Job's reply that also praises the power and greatness of God, then this speech was originally a full-length response to a disturbing question that Job raised in answer to Bildad's first speech (session 7). Job protested that God's wisdom is so profound and his power so vast, that mere mortals could never prove their innocence before God. "Though I were innocent, I could not answer him," Job complained. God could always find something that he could have done differently or better, and God could use his superior power to crush any protest.

In reply to this argument, which has perhaps been troubling him ever since Job raised it, Bildad now reasserts God's wisdom and power, using language very reminiscent of Job's. (For example, he describes how God conquered the chaos monster Rahab, how he makes pillars quake and spreads out the skies, etc.) But Bildad draws a different conclusion. The problem, he says, isn't how mortals can *prove* their innocence; they simply can't *be* innocent in the first place, not in the sight of an all-knowing, all-powerful God. And so—continuing the repartee that has run all the way through the exchange of speeches—Bildad suggests that Job's own words ultimately condemn him.

⮎ If God does want to punish even the slightest infraction, then it's a serious problem for us that God knows everything we think, say, and do, and that his power is inescapable. However, if God is prepared to pardon and forgive, then it's actually comforting to acknowledge his comprehensive knowledge and supreme power, because these mean that we are always under his watchful care and protection. In other words, our beliefs about the implications of God's wisdom and power depend on our understanding of his character. Bildad believes in a stern, punitive God. But if God is essentially gracious and kind instead, what are the implications of Bildad's accurate observations:

> That nothing is hidden from God, not even in the depths of the sea or in the realm of the dead?
> That God wants to establish order and harmony throughout the creation?
> That even the greatest things we're aware of God doing are only the "outer fringe of his works"?

2 Only a brief portion of Job's original reply to Bildad's third speech appears to have been preserved in the book as we know it today: an opening rebuke of the friends, plus a characteristic impassioned defense of Job's innocence. Amazingly, Job swears by God ("as surely as God lives") that he is innocent, even though he has to describe him as "God . . . who has denied me justice, the Almighty, who has made my life bitter." Despite all that has happened to him without explanation, Job still maintains his trust in God.

⮑ What do you think Job would tell you in reply if you asked him, "How can you consider God trustworthy enough to guarantee an oath when you believe he's denied you justice?"

3 If the last part of Job's reply to Bildad in the current text of the book was originally spoken by Zophar, then he would have intended it as a conclusion to all three rounds of speeches: "I will teach you about the power of God; the ways of the Almighty I will not conceal. You have all seen this yourselves. Why then this meaningless talk?" Zophar would be addressing both Job and the other two friends when he suggests that their entire extended conversation has been "meaningless" (or "futile"). As far as he's concerned, the position the friends have taken right from the start represents a self-evident truth about God and the world, and there has been no point arguing about it all this time. God punishes and destroys the wicked, and given what Job has suffered, he must be among them. (The depiction here of how the wicked are destroyed once again includes details that are pointedly aimed at Job: the death of all one's children, the sudden loss of wealth, devastation brought by strong winds, etc.)

If these words did originally belong to Zophar, then they show that he, Eliphaz, and Bildad have wasted a priceless opportunity to explore some of the most profound questions of human existence with a godly friend who's a daring original thinker. They have simply asserted their own conventional position and held to it inflexibly no matter how much Job has probed, challenged, and critiqued it.

⮑ Has your understanding of God and the world changed and grown as you've read and discussed the exchange of speeches between Job and his friends? If so, in what ways?

WHERE CAN WISDOM BE FOUND?

Book of Job > Interlude: The Hymn to Wisdom

INTRODUCTION

About halfway through the book of Job, just after the exchange of speeches ends between Job and his friends, there's an interlude or break in the action. In this interlude a voice other than one of the characters speaks. It addresses the audience in the language of their own time (for example, calling God *Elohim* rather than *Eloah* as the characters do in their earlier setting). This material is often called the Hymn to Wisdom.

Some interpreters suggest that in ancient times, when the book of Job would have been customarily read out loud, the Hymn to Wisdom was sung while the rest was spoken. Others suggest that the book may have been presented as a play and that a chorus came on stage to speak the hymn in unison. Whatever the case, this material does call for a presentation that distinguishes its voice from the voices of the regular characters.

The stately cadence of the hymn provides a welcome respite after the wrangling between Job and his friends. Its message, that God alone knows the way to wisdom, helps prepare listeners for the remaining episodes and the conclusion of the book.

READING

Have a member of your group read the Hymn to Wisdom out loud, beginning with "There is a mine for silver and a place where gold is refined" and ending with "The fear of the Lord*—that is wisdom, and to shun evil is understanding." Note how the hymn is divided into three sections by a refrain that's repeated twice: "Where can wisdom be found? Where does understanding dwell?"

DISCUSSION

1 It was common in the wisdom tradition of the ancient world to say that wisdom was worth more than precious metals or jewels and that a person should search for it as diligently as someone digging for those valuable commodities. The book of Proverbs, for example, a collection of wise sayings that were passed down within the nation of Israel, says, "Blessed are those who find wisdom, those who gain understanding, for she is more profitable than silver and yields better returns than gold. She is more precious than rubies; nothing you desire can compare with her." It says similarly, "If you call out for insight and cry aloud for understanding, and if you look for it as for silver and search for it as for hidden treasure, then you will understand the fear of the LORD and find the knowledge of God."

The Hymn to Wisdom uses this same imagery. Its opening section offers an elaborate description—fascinating from our perspective because it depicts ancient mining techniques—of how people go to the remotest parts of the earth and tunnel to great depths to find gold, silver, and precious stones. Its second section offers a fabulous list of precious metals and jewels but insists that wisdom is more valuable than all of them. Readers of the book would expect a conventional conclusion such as, "If you search for wisdom just as

---

* The Hebrew term used here is *Adonai*, "Master," which pious Jews came to substitute for the divine name *Yahweh* when they read aloud from the Scriptures. This is one more suggestion that Job was written, or at least finalized, at a relatively later point in Israel's history. In keeping with the common practice of English Bible translators, "Lord" for *Adonai* is not written in large and small caps the way "LORD" for *Yahweh* is.

diligently, you will find it as your reward." Instead, the hymn poses a question: "But where can wisdom be found?" Even though human ingenuity can bring such treasures out of the depths of the earth, people still don't know the way to wisdom; only God does. The book has already been undermining an overconfidence in human understanding by demonstrating the deficiencies of the friends' conventional outlook. Now it says explicitly that even the most learned and thoughtful of people will never understand human existence comprehensively.

➲ Have you ever had an experience when it cost you something to learn a lesson, but the lesson was so valuable and important that you felt it was worth the cost? If so, share your experience with the group.

➲ In the centuries since the book of Job was written, science and technology have advanced to an extent that its author might never have dreamed possible. Humans have now looked into the farthest reaches of outer space and mapped the ocean floors. Do you think that science and technology will someday explain everything about the universe? Or will there always be some questions about life that remain beyond human investigation and understanding?

2 The Hymn to Wisdom insists that wisdom isn't to be found anywhere that humans *can* look on their own, even if they travel to the farthest ends of the earth and dig deep beneath it. The hymn also says that wisdom isn't to be found in those places where humans *can't* look: the depths of the sea (unfathomable at the time) and the abode of the dead. "The sea says, 'It is not with me.' . . . Destruction and Death say, 'Only a rumor of it has reached our ears.'" These same two realms have just been mentioned in Job's reply to Bildad's third speech (in the section that might have originally been spoken by Bildad himself) as places that God fully understands and controls. This connection helps integrate the Hymn to Wisdom into the book at this point. It also reinforces the message that even the parts of the created world that are beyond human grasp don't hold some secret that, if disclosed, would nullify what we believe about God based on the experience we do have of the creation around us.

⮑ A friend of yours has been reading some popular scientific literature on the idea of multiple parallel universes. This friend says to you, "You believe in God and Jesus and all that because you live in this universe, but if you could step into one of those other universes, you'd discover that things really don't work the way you think." How do you respond?

3 The Hymn to Wisdom concludes by insisting that only God knows the way to wisdom, since he alone understands every aspect of the creation comprehensively. It ends with God speaking and explaining, "The fear of the Lord—that is wisdom, and to shun evil is understanding." This sounds at first very much like the conventional teaching of the ancient wisdom tradition. The book of Proverbs says near its outset, for example, "The fear of the LORD is the beginning of wisdom." But there is a subtle difference. The statement in Proverbs, in the context of that book, means that if a person "fears the LORD" (that is, if they don't dare to do anything that they know is wrong), then this will lead them, over time, into a deep understanding of life—the fear of the LORD is the *beginning* of wisdom. But the statement here must be taken somewhat differently in the context of this unconventional book, particularly since it echoes precisely the opening description of Job himself: He "feared God and shunned evil." It likely means that turning away from evil is the wise and proper course in life—the fear of the Lord *is* wisdom—even if, as in Job's case, things don't go the way a person expects and they never completely understand why.

⮑ If you're a follower of Jesus, what's your biggest unanswered question about why something has happened to you, or hasn't happened for you, even though you were living the way you thought you should? What do you think of the idea that you might not ever get an answer to this question but that you should just keep living in a way that honors God?

JOB DESCRIBES THE LOSSES HE'S SUFFERED

INTRODUCTION

After the Hymn to Wisdom, the book of Job moves into a new phase. The friends were functioning like a grand jury, weighing Job's claim that he had a case to bring against God. Even though they concluded that he didn't (they were never really open to the possibility in the first place), Job now takes God to court anyway. And so the trial begins. The opposing party is nowhere to be found, and no impartial referee has been identified, but Job proceeds with his case. In eloquent language that evokes the images of light and darkness, water and vegetation, and weapons of war that recurred throughout the exchange of speeches, Job swears out an affidavit that he is innocent of the crimes for which he is apparently already being punished. (Because of the length of this affidavit, we will consider it in this session and the following one.)

READING

Have someone read the first part of Job's affidavit, in which he describes the reputation and respect he once enjoyed in the community, beginning with "How I long for the months gone by, for the days when God watched over me" and ending with "I dwelt as a king among his troops; I was like one who comforts mourners."

Then have someone read the next part, in which Job describes how even the lowest ruffians in the community now treat him with contempt, beginning with "But now they mock me, men younger than I, whose fathers I would have disdained to put with my sheep dogs" and ending with "Terrors overwhelm me; my dignity is driven away as by the wind, my safety vanishes like a cloud."

Then have someone read the next part, in which Job laments his physical sufferings, beginning with "And now my life ebbs away; days of suffering grip me" and ending with "My lyre is tuned to mourning, and my pipe to the sound of wailing."

(We will consider the final part of the affidavit, in which Job guarantees his claim of innocence with a series of oaths, in the next session.)

DISCUSSION

1 In trials today, the public and jury may become so accustomed to seeing the defendant in handcuffs and prison garb that it's difficult for them to think of him or her as an honest citizen. And so a defense lawyer will often begin by introducing evidence of the defendant's previous status and the contributions they've made to society, and by calling character witnesses.

In the same way, Job begins his affidavit by recalling his former standing in the community. While the opening narrative of the book depicts Job as "the greatest man among all the people of the East" by describing his wealth and possessions, here Job portrays his former position in terms of the reputation he achieved and the respect with which he was treated. When he gave his opinion on a matter, this was the last word on the subject. He was known specifically at the city gate, where important community concerns were debated and disputes were settled, as someone who recognized the claims of the poor, weak, and needy and knew how to get justice for them. This same consideration, Job implies, should be accorded to him as well.

⮑ Is there someone you know whose reputation would make you doubt that they had actually committed a crime if they were accused of one? Who is this person, and what makes you trust in their character and integrity to this extent?

⮑ How do the people of your society typically measure and evaluate their level of personal success: Is it by how much money they make? The position they obtain? How much celebrity they achieve? Something else? If you believed that the true measure of a person's accomplishments was the reputation they earned for integrity and good judgment, would this make your values, priorities, and activities any different from what they are now? If so, how?

2 In Job's society, people show deference to others of greater age and stature. He has just described how younger men used to make way for him and older ones would stand up to show their respect. Even the "chief men" would fall silent to let him speak. (We'll soon see this kind of deference illustrated within the book itself, as Elihu explains why he has waited to speak.) The society is governed by considerations of honor and shame; it's important for each person to know their place and not disgrace themselves by stepping outside of it.

At the bottom of the social scale is a band of shiftless young men who lead a subsistence existence in the wastelands. Their emaciated bodies are no longer fit for honest work, and they're chased away whenever they approach civilized society. Job describes them literally as "sons of fools" and "sons of those without a name." Ordinarily people like this wouldn't dare say a word against him. But now they sing mocking songs about him and use his name as a curse word. This, Job explains, is the loss he has suffered because of what God has done to him. Once respected and honored by the greatest people in his community, he's now treated with contempt by the worst.

➲ You're a young adult who's just gotten a job as a clerk in a department store. The manager is training you and instructs you to address customers by their first names (which you can read off their credit cards) when thanking them for their purchases. This, the manager says, will give the transaction "that personal touch." One of your first customers is a former teacher of yours, a woman in her sixties who has just retired after a distinguished career. The manager is standing a few feet away, watching and listening. Do you address this customer by her first name?

➲ In seeking damages against God in this lawsuit, why do you think Job measures his loss in terms of his reputation, rather than in terms of his wealth?

3 Having described the loss he has suffered, Job now makes a formal charge against the person he considers responsible—God. Job has not addressed God directly since the middle of the second round of speeches, but he does so again here. He argues that any decent person would help someone who was in need. Since he personally has a long history of helping such people, he'd expect that when he was in trouble himself, God, at least, would come to his aid. But instead, God has picked him up by the scruff of the neck and tossed him to the ground. As a result, while Job was once sure that he would die comfortably in his own home, now he's living instead in the mud and dust, just like the shiftless young men who live in the "dry stream beds." Like them, he's been driven from respectable society, in his case because of his disfiguring skin disease (which makes him ceremonially unclean). He describes it again here in vivid detail. All of this, he says, has happened because God has turned on him "ruthlessly."

When Job speaks about God in this way, it may appear that he's not honoring his own society's code of showing deference to those of greater age and stature. But Job is showing a paradoxical kind of respect for God here. As we've seen, he continues to trust him. Job believes that if he can just get an impartial hearing at which he can explain how God has been treating him unfairly, God will recognize and admit this and make things right. This actually expresses confidence in God's character and integrity.

> ⮑ In private prayer or in conversations with your friends, have you ever accused God the way Job does here? Do you think that Job's actions are presented to us in the Scriptures as a model of something that's acceptable, so long as the same kind of confidence in God's character underlies any accusations we might make?

JOB GUARANTEES HIS INNOCENCE WITH A SEVENFOLD OATH

Book of Job > Job's Affidavit, continued

INTRODUCTION

After describing the damages he's suffered and demanding that God answer for them, Job concludes his affidavit by swearing to his own innocence. In a series of oaths, he calls down curses upon himself if he has truly done the kind of things his friends have accused him of doing. Job is pursuing a brilliant legal strategy. In the ancient world, oaths like these were more than just a court formality guaranteeing truthful testimony. People expected that the curses named would actually fall upon the person if they were guilty. So God must now answer Job in some way. If God does not carry out the curses to show that Job is guilty, then he will be giving an implied verdict of "innocent."

This part of the affidavit follows the "six, yes, seven" pattern that was a favorite in Hebrew literature. (In his first speech, for example, Eliphaz told Job, "From six calamities [God] will rescue you; in seven no harm will touch you.") After a brief prologue, Job swears out six oaths; then he says he is signing his defense, and he challenges God to respond; and finally he swears a seventh oath.

Job's "signature" may simply be a gesture he makes to dramatize that he can guarantee his innocence. It's possible, however, that someone has been recording his affidavit and that he literally signs it at this point. (As we'll see in the next session, there are actually more people present than just Job and his friends.) It's also possible that by putting his avowal of innocence in writing (whether literally or figuratively), Job is challenging God to acquit him in writing, not just implicitly, if he won't activate the curses. The Hebrew text reads literally, "Let the other party in my *rîb* write a document," which could actually mean a written declaration of innocence that Job would proudly wear and display.

READING

Have people take turns reading these parts of Job's affidavit out loud, starting at the places indicated:

- Prologue: "I made a covenant with my eyes . . ."
- Oath 1: "If I have walked with falsehood or my foot has hurried after deceit . . ."
- Oath 2: "If my heart has been enticed by a woman, or if I have lurked at my neighbor's door . . ."
- Oath 3: "If I have denied justice to any of my servants, whether male or female . . ."
- Oath 4: "If I have denied the desires of the poor or let the eyes of the widow grow weary . . ."
- Oath 5: "If I have put my trust in gold or said to pure gold, 'You are my security' . . ."
- Oath 6: "If I have rejoiced at my enemy's misfortune or gloated over the trouble that came to him . . ."
- Guarantee: "Oh, that I had someone to hear me! I sign now my defense . . ."
- Oath 7: "If my land cries out against me and all its furrows are wet with tears . . ." (concluding with "The words of Job are ended").

DISCUSSION

1 The seven oaths all follow a similar pattern. Job first describes some wrong thing he might have done. In many cases, it's something the friends have said or implied he is guilty of. Then he calls a curse down upon himself if he has actually done this thing. The punishment usually fits the crime, for example, "If I have raised my hand against the fatherless . . . let my arm fall from the shoulder, let it be broken off at the joint." (In a few cases, Job doesn't mention a specific punishment; he just says it would be right for God to punish him for this action.)

⮑ Form several smaller teams within your group and assign all of the seven oaths to various teams. Have the teams investigate the following questions and then report their answers back to the group as a whole:

    a. What wrong action or actions does this oath describe?

    b. Have the friends accused Job of doing something like this? If so, when? If not, is Job describing something the friends are doing wrong? (There are some suggested answers to this question at the end of this session.)

    c. What penalty, if any, does Job say he should suffer if he's actually guilty?

    d. How does the punishment, if specified, fit the crime?

    e. What would be the contemporary equivalent of the wrong that Job describes? Give several examples if you can.

    f. Can you sum up the message of this oath in one sentence as an ethical principle? (That is, not as a rule to follow, but as a way of "fearing God and shunning evil.")

2 In his prologue to this series of oaths, Job says that God brings ruin to the wicked and disaster on those who do wrong. But when speaking with his friends, he argued that God doesn't necessarily punish the wicked in this life. (Job even suggested at one point, when pushed to an extreme, that the wicked generally go unpunished.) How can we explain this apparent contradiction? What Job means here is that he will be speaking this series of oaths as a devout person who wants God to punish *him* if he actually is guilty of these things. If Job didn't believe God would do this, he could insincerely call these curses down on himself without really fearing any punishment. And asking God to punish him if he is guilty is still quite different from granting the friends' reverse premise, that if it appears a person is being punished, they must be guilty of something.

⟳ Do you believe that God can and does punish people in this life in specific ways for particular offenses, to the extent that you could with integrity guarantee your innocence by saying, "If I have done this wrong thing, then may God punish me in this fitting way"? Explain.

3 Job has not been accused of sexual impropriety at any point, but he still swears, in the second oath, that he's innocent of this kind of wrongdoing. (He even starts to explain, before he begins the whole series of oaths, about the disciplines he has built into his life to guard against lust: "I made a covenant with my eyes not to look lustfully at a young woman.") But the curse Job invokes as part of this second oath seems to punish his wife rather than himself: If he's taken another man's wife, then may someone else take his wife. Job's language suggests that she would specifically become a concubine, that is, a female slave and secondary wife to another man. While this would no doubt be painful and humiliating for Job, it would be far worse for his wife.

⟳ Which of the following do you think best explains what's going on here?

a. Job has been miffed at his wife ever since she told him to "curse God and die." This is payback time.

b. In this patriarchal culture, women were regarded as little better than property. For Job, having another man take his wife would be like someone else eating his crops. Here the Bible is presenting a general portrait of a righteous person within the context of this culture. The Bible's critique of the treatment of women within patriarchal cultures unfolds over the length of its whole story and in the aftermath of that story, as it has influenced history.

c. Job is so certain he's lived a righteous life that he's willing to invoke curses that affect not only himself but also those he loves, because he knows the curses will never come into effect.

Suggested answers to discussion point 1 in section 2:

Oath 1: Bildad, in his second speech, and Eliphaz, in his third speech, accused Job of becoming rich by exploiting the poor. Bildad said of the wicked, "His own hands must give back his wealth." Job says here, "If I have walked with falsehood . . . may others eat what I have sown."

Oath 2: The friends have not accused Job of adultery.

Oath 3: Job may be saying the friends should have granted him a hearing.

Oath 4: In his third speech, Eliphaz told Job, "You sent widows away empty-handed and broke the strength of the fatherless."

Oath 5: In that same speech, Eliphaz told Job, "If you . . . assign your nuggets to the dust . . . then the Almighty will be your gold."

Oath 6: Job has accused his friends of not being sympathetic to him in his misfortunes. Eliphaz, again in his third speech, accused Job of thinking he could hide from God.

Oath 7: This may also be a response to the accusation that Job has exploited the poor.

ELIHU INSISTS THAT GOD HAS ALREADY BEEN ANSWERING JOB

Book of Job > Elihu > First Speech

INTRODUCTION

After Job concludes his affidavit by swearing to his innocence, the book springs yet another of its characteristic surprises. To this point there has been little indication that anyone except Job and his three friends have been sitting together talking. But now we discover that at least one other person (perhaps along with many others) has been listening to their whole conversation. Since the friends have "found no way to refute Job," a younger man named Elihu speaks up.

Elihu is introduced as the "son of Barakel the Buzite, of the family of Ram." These are all Hebrew names, suggesting that Elihu is related to Abraham, the ancestor of the Israelites, although it can't be determined how close a relative he is. Elihu and his clan may have been nomadic herders, like the rest of the Hebrews at this time. The book of Job is set in the Arabian desert to the east of Israel, so Elihu would either have been staying in that region already, or else like the friends, he came there when he heard about Job's misfortunes.

The author has taken care, and perhaps some delight as well, in character-izing Elihu as long-winded and brash, in contrast with the more dignified way the friends are portrayed. Elihu poses as a daring, avant-garde thinker, but his arguments lack coherence and sometimes even seem to contradict one another. His sudden appearance and extended ramblings feel like such an interruption in the book that many interpreters wonder whether this character wasn't actually added later by a different author. (They note that he's not mentioned in the opening or closing narratives.) But other interpreters argue that Elihu fits well within the book's overall structure and thematic development. His character, which the original audience would find comical at times, provides some light relief as Job's proceeding against God nears an inevitable showdown. His speeches also create a delay between Job's sworn affidavit and God's ultimate response, assuring readers that Job hasn't forced God to respond to him at a particular time or in a particular way. Most significantly, as we'll see, at times Elihu does speak for the author of the book, articulating themes that help bring its overall argument to its conclusion.

As expected in this culture, Elihu has deferred to those of greater age and stature, allowing them to speak without interruption. But now that the friends have fallen silent, he seizes the opening. After an elaborate explanation of why he hasn't spoken before and why he's speaking now (Elihu is clearly someone who likes to hear the sound of his own voice), he shares his own thoughts about Job's situation. Elihu makes a series of four speeches. We'll consider them over the next three sessions, beginning in this session with the first one.

The three friends have argued, unsuccessfully, that Job doesn't have a valid case to bring against God. In this first part of his speech, Elihu takes a different tack. He insists that the opposing party has already answered the charges against him, so there's no need to continue the proceedings: "Why do you complain [*ríb*] to him," he asks Job, "that he does not answer for any of his actions?" (See NIV translators' note for this reading.) "For God does speak," Elihu insists, "now one way, now another—though no one perceives it." He then describes the ways in which, as he sees it, God has already been answering Job's questions about what has happened to him.

READING

Have someone read the short narrative that introduces Elihu.

Then have someone read Elihu's first speech, beginning with "I am young in years, and you are old" and ending with "Listen to me; be silent, and I will teach you wisdom." The person who portrays Elihu shouldn't hesitate to speak in a theatrical and self-assured way, in keeping with his character.

DISCUSSION

1 Elihu argues that God has already been answering Job in two ways. First, he observes, God may speak to people in a dream or "vision of the night" and "terrify them with warnings, to turn them from wrongdoing." Job had said to God, in his reply to Eliphaz's first speech, "You frighten me with dreams and terrify me with visions," so Elihu is closely echoing Job's own words. He's suggesting that, by his own admission, Job has already been hearing back from God. Job was really trying to say that God was giving him no rest, day or night, but Elihu believes that the dreams were in fact God speaking to him and telling him to change his ways.

According to Elihu, the second way God speaks to people, even if they don't always realize it, is through their suffering itself. Still echoing Job's own words, Elihu observes, "Someone may be chastened on a bed of pain with constant distress in their bones." The word translated "chasten" here means to correct, reprove, or admonish. Once again, God's purpose is not so much to punish Job as to warn and correct him.

And so, as far as Elihu is concerned, through these two means God has already answered Job's questions about why all these things have happened to him.

⮑ Whether or not Elihu is correctly applying his insights to Job's particular situation, we can still consider them as potentially valid general truths. Have you ever had a dream that helped you realize you were on the wrong course and needed to take a different one? What role, if any, do you think God played in giving you this dream?

⮑ C. S. Lewis wrote in *The Problem of Pain*, "God whispers to us in our pleasures, speaks in our conscience, but shouts in our pain: it is His megaphone to rouse a deaf world."* If God is truly a loving God, is it consistent with his character to inflict pain on someone in order to get their attention? Do you believe that God has ever done this with you? (If so, tell your story to the group if you can.) Would it be wise, as a general rule, to say to people in pain, "God must be trying to get your attention"?

2 Elihu describes how God might send an "angel" or "messenger" to a person he was chastising with pain. The word translated "angel" here is the general Hebrew term for someone who brings news, information, or instructions from one person to another. In most English versions of the Bible, this term is translated "messenger" when it refers to a human, and "angel" when it refers to a being sent by God. The second term is actually the same one that Job used in his reply to Eliphaz's second speech when he spoke of an "intercessor" who would be a witness and advocate for him "on high."

The situation Elihu is describing here reflects the practice in this culture of having go-betweens conduct business between people of greatly differing stations. For example, a young man who wanted to marry a young woman would not approach her father himself. Rather, the young man's own father, or his older brother, would go and speak for him. God wants to be reconciled with the person he is chastening with pain, so he sends a suitable go-between to "tell them how to be upright." If he receives a positive report from this representative, Elihu explains, God may be gracious and say, "Spare them from going down to the pit; I have found a ransom." (The NIV translation portrays the messenger as the speaker of these words, but the phrase "to God" is not actually in the original text, so the speaker could just as well be God himself. That possibility is well suited to Elihu's overall argument, that God sent the deadly disease as a warning but ultimately wants to turn the person from their wrongdoing and spare them.) The term "ransom" refers to anything that gives an offended party satisfaction and restores a broken relationship. This could be a payment for damages suffered or, as appears likely in this case, the word of an impartial mediator that the offending party has recognized their fault and is now prepared to deal honestly and fairly.

---

* C. S. Lewis, *The Problem of Pain* (1940; San Francisco: HarperSanFrancisco, 2001), 91.

◌ Does this explanation of the role of a go-between in the biblical culture help you understand anything more about why God sent Jesus to the world in the form of a human in order to bring about reconciliation between himself and the human race? If so, share your insights with the group.

◌ Followers of Jesus today are often encouraged to approach God boldly, even familiarly, with their requests and concerns. Do you think they should instead show deference to God's infinitely higher standing and ask Jesus to intercede for them, or at least pray more intentionally in Jesus' name? Or should followers of Jesus see themselves as sons and daughters of God who can always go directly into their heavenly Father's presence?

3 The friends insisted in all of their speeches that Job should not challenge the received wisdom passed down through the generations. But Elihu suggests a radically different notion: "It is the spirit in a person, the breath of the Almighty, that gives them understanding. It is not only the old who are wise, not only the aged who understand what is right." As the NIV translators' note indicates, "spirit" here could also be translated "Spirit," that is, God's Spirit. Elihu believes that whatever their age or standing, a Spirit-inspired person—and he considers himself to be one—is capable of keen, penetrating insights that can transcend even the wisdom of a mind steeped in learning and tradition.

◌ What do you think of Elihu's claim here: Is there a spiritual gift of insight or knowledge that's equal or superior to the fruits of learning and the wisdom of experience?

◌ Can you remember a time when you were glad you listened to the ideas of a person who seemed like an unlikely source of guidance? If so, describe what happened briefly for the group. Why did you, or a group you were part of, need good advice? Why might you have not listened to this person: Were they young? Less educated? New to the group? What happened in the end?

ELIHU CHALLENGES JOB TO RESPECT GOD'S AUTHORITY

Book of Job > Elihu's Second and Third Speeches

INTRODUCTION

At the end of his first speech, Elihu invites Job to respond to him as he responded to each of the friends. But for some reason, Job doesn't reply. (Perhaps it is because Elihu is so eager to keep talking that Job just lets him go on: Elihu says, "If you have anything to say, answer me . . . But if not, then listen to me; be silent, and I will teach you wisdom.") So Elihu continues sharing his own perspectives on Job's situation. We'll consider his second and third speeches in this session.

READING AND DISCUSSION

1 Have someone read Elihu's second speech, beginning with "Hear my words, you wise men; listen to me, you men of learning" and ending with "Scornfully he claps his hands among us and multiplies his words against God."

In his first speech, Elihu insisted that God had already answered Job, so there was no need for any further proceedings. Now in this second speech Elihu offers a further argument: God never needs to hold a trial in the first place. He already knows the facts and can determine a person's guilt or innocence. So there's no reason for Job to believe that a trial is even necessary.

Elihu explains that God sees and knows everything that people do ("His eyes are on the ways of mortals; he sees their every step") and that he judges human actions with perfect accuracy ("It is unthinkable that God would do wrong, that the Almighty would pervert justice"). These same things are asserted frequently throughout the biblical wisdom tradition. However, Elihu draws a unique conclusion here: Because God is all-knowing and perfectly just, he executes summary justice without open proceedings: "God has no need to examine people further, that they should come before him for judgment. *Without inquiry* he shatters the mighty and sets up others in their place." Therefore, if God "remains silent" (that is, if he doesn't answer for his actions), "who can condemn him?" God is not accountable to any higher authority: "Who appointed him over the earth? Who put him in charge of the whole world?" So he certainly doesn't need to answer to a mere mortal like Job.

> ⮑ Even if God doesn't need to hold trials to establish the facts and determine guilt or innocence, would some other purposes be served if God explained to people, at least to some extent, the reasons behind his judgments? What would those purposes be? If you're familiar with other parts of the Bible, do you see God doing this at any point?

2 Elihu considers the case of a person who realizes they're being punished by God and who says, "I am guilty but will offend no more . . . If I have done wrong, I will not do so again." Elihu insists that even a person like this can't ask God to reduce their punishment: "Should God then reward you on your terms, when you refuse to repent?" The original Hebrew reads simply, ". . . when you refuse?" The term that's used, *ma'as*, is an important one in the book of Job. It means to disdain something, to treat something as if it had little worth or value. For example, when complaining about his loss of standing, Job described how he was being treated disrespectfully by young men whose fathers he would have *disdained* to put with his sheep dogs. The verb can be used with an object, as when Job says in his first reply to Bildad,

"I *despise* my own life." But it can also be used without an object, which then has to be inferred from the context, as when Job says in his first reply to Eliphaz, "I *despise*, I would not live forever," meaning once again that he despises his own life.

Elihu is using the term here without stating its object, but his meaning can be inferred from the context: "Should God then reward you [that is, compensate you] on your terms, when you *disdain* [his terms]?" Elihu insists to Job, "You must choose" (NIV "decide") whether you're willing to engage God on his own terms or whether you're going to insist on dealing with God on yours. The use of the significant term *ma'as* shows that at this point, despite his long ramblings, Elihu is now speaking for the author of the book and presenting its central challenge to all of its readers: You must make the same choice yourself. This imperative will be presented even more vividly as the book reaches its culmination.

Within the immediate context of this speech, however, Elihu's specific argument is that in seeking a lighter punishment, Job is actually questioning God's judicial authority and decrees, for which God is accountable to no one. So why should God give in to this? The ironic implications are that Job couldn't change anything about his situation even if he took to heart the warning Elihu said God was sending him through his terrifying dreams and physical pains. Job is just supposed to accept God's judgment, without pleading for mercy on the basis of his good behavior.

⮑ What do you think: If we realize from the consequences of our actions that a course we're taking is wrong, and if we choose a better one instead, can we then legitimately ask God to relieve some of the consequences of the former course? Explain.

3 Have someone read Elihu's third speech, beginning with "Do you think this is just? You say, 'I am in the right, not God'" and ending with "So Job opens his mouth with empty talk; without knowledge he multiplies words."

In his first two speeches, Elihu addressed Job's claim that God owed him a hearing. Now, in this third speech, he responds to two further things that Job said in response to the friends.

To begin with, Elihu addresses Job's repeated complaint that he shouldn't be suffering so much since he's innocent—in other words, he deserves to be treated better. In his first reply to Eliphaz, Job insisted that nothing he might have done wrong had taken anything away from God, so there was no need for God to watch him closely and punish the slightest infraction. Eliphaz countered, in his third speech, that nothing Job might have done right had added anything to God, either, so God didn't owe him any favors. Elihu agrees with Eliphaz here. He describes God as so far above the world that he's unaffected by human goodness. God is therefore under no constraint to show special favors to the righteous. So even if Job is innocent, as he claims (and Elihu has already declared that he isn't), he has no grounds for complaint.

⮑ Even if human goodness doesn't put God under any kind of obligation, do you think God is more positively disposed towards people who are trying to live as he desires? If so, is God more likely to arrange circumstances in their favor? Explain.

4 But Elihu also agrees with Job, that God is put under no constraint by human wickedness, either, and this leads into his next argument in this third speech. Elihu attempts to reconcile his earlier depiction of God as the all-seeing, all-powerful judge of the world with Job's repeated observation—which he does not dispute—that all over the world innocent people are oppressed by the wicked but God doesn't do anything about it.

Elihu argues that when God doesn't answer people's cries for deliverance, it's because these are insincere. People only want relief from their desperate circumstances. When they call to God, even when they're basically innocent victims of oppression, they're still not really acknowledging him as their maker and recognizing him as the giver of good gifts such as music and learning. So "God does not listen to their empty plea." Job, he concludes, has even less reason to expect that God will listen to him, since he's someone who has openly questioned God's character. "How much less, then, will he listen when you say that you do not see him . . ."

⮑ What do you think would happen if, the next time you found yourself in a difficult situation, you said sincerely to God, "I was going to ask you to get me out of this mess, but then I got to thinking what an amazing person you must be, since you created the beauty of this world and gave us the gifts of art and music and literature, so all I want to ask is to get to know you better"?

ELIHU COMPARES GOD'S POWER TO AN APPROACHING STORM

INTRODUCTION

For a younger man who has claimed divine inspiration for his bold ideas, Elihu begins his fourth speech in a disappointingly conventional way. He sounds just like the friends when he first recounts the blessings of the righteous and the troubles of the wicked and then appeals to Job to abandon his guilty ways. It's as if this would-be daring thinker has run out of provocative ideas and needs to fall back on the stock themes of his culture to finish his series of speeches.

However, as he then turns to describe God's greatness and power (which are also common themes of the wisdom tradition), his words take on a new energy. As he's describing how God cares for the earth by watering it, he begins to describe a thunderstorm. Readers suddenly realize, in another of the surprises the book loves to spring, that an actual storm is brewing. Elihu is weaving into his speech what he sees as it approaches: "*See* how he scatters his lightning about him . . . *Listen! Listen* to the roar of his voice . . . He thunders with his majestic voice." Elihu suggested in his first speech that God's spirit, the "breath of the Almighty," might inspire even a younger, less experienced person to speak profound truths, and the winds of the approaching storm that he describes as the "breath of God" seem to be inspiring his suddenly eloquent and penetrating insights in the rest of this speech.

As the storm looms overhead and erupts in a downpour, driving everyone to shelter, Elihu concludes his speech with a wisdom interrogation. He peppers Job with questions about the workings of the universe ("Do you know how God controls the clouds and makes his lightning flash?") to get Job to consider whether he really wants to face God in a court case. His language echoes the conclusion of the Hymn to Wisdom and anticipates how the book itself will end. This is one of the places where the author's voice is heard most clearly.

READING

Have someone read Elihu's fourth speech, beginning with "Bear with me a little longer and I will show you that there is more to be said in God's behalf" and ending with "Therefore, people revere him, for does he not have regard for all the wise in heart?" Choose a reader who has good expression and have them dramatize the arrival of the storm (for example, pointing when Elihu says, "See," clutching a fist to their chest when he says, "My heart pounds," etc.).

DISCUSSION

1 Even though the first part of this speech is conventional in many respects, it does address one more important question that Job raised in his exchange with the friends. Job suggested that God might be using his superior power and knowledge to manipulate our relationship with him to his own advantage, without us realizing it or being able to do anything about it. Elihu counters that "God is mighty, but *despises* no one." The term is the significant *ma'as*, and it is actually used without an object. The meaning that can be inferred from the context is, "God is mighty, but does not despise [those who are not mighty] . . . He gives the afflicted their rights." In other words, for God, might is not right; right is right. God's character qualities of generosity and even humility enable him to recognize the worth of people in the lowest circumstances and lead him to defend their dignity.

⤳ Have you ever met people who didn't want to be friends with other people if they weren't like them in certain ways? Have you met others who were genuinely welcoming of others no matter what their background or status? Does the contrast between these two kinds of people help you understand the character quality of God that Elihu describes here, "God is mighty, but does not despise?"

⤳ What would it mean to you if it were really true that God didn't consider his great superiority in wisdom, power, and holiness an obstacle to a relationship with you? What if God wouldn't exploit this difference within the relationship?

2 As Elihu describes the power of God through the features of the approaching storm, he implicitly also depicts the qualities of God. For example, he says that God's lightning "bathes the depths of the sea"—in other words, that his lightning is so bright it illuminates even the bottom of the ocean. While this is not literally true, it symbolically illustrates the truth proclaimed in the Hymn to Wisdom and at the end of the exchange of speeches, that while the ocean depths are inaccessible to people, God knows what lies there. So the lightning is symbolic of his comprehensive knowledge. (By contrast, Elihu says that humans are in "darkness.") Similarly, he says that God "brings the clouds to punish people, or to water his earth and show his love." The thunder and lightning represent God's justice, the rains represent his goodness and care.

⤳ What's the most powerful and moving way you've experienced God's greatness through some aspect of creation? As you think back over this experience, what qualities of God does it disclose?

3 Elihu describes how a downpour or a snowstorm leads animals to take cover and "stops all people from their labor." Such events create a natural Sabbath, when everyone has to step back from their daily work and reflect on God's power and goodness as the Creator.

⊃ If you live in a colder climate, has it ever snowed so heavily that normal work and travel were impossible for several days? What did you do during this time? Did you relate to the people around you any differently? If you live in a different type of climate, what other kinds of weather conditions might interrupt normal activities in this same way? Despite the dangers of extreme weather, were you able to enjoy something of a natural Sabbath?

As Elihu winds down his long speech, the horizon is clearing and the sun appears in the distance, its golden rays contrasting vividly with the dark clouds still looming overhead. Using yet another natural element to describe God's power and qualities, Elihu says that like the blinding sun, God is coming in "awesome majesty" out of the "north" (the mythic abode of divine beings in the ancient world). Is this going to be a glorious and peaceful sunny evening after a stormy day? Or is something stirring within that storm cloud . . .

THE LORD PORTRAYS A WILD WORLD OUTSIDE THE REALM OF HUMANITY

Book of Job > The LORD's First Speech
Book of Job > Job's Reply to the LORD's First Speech

INTRODUCTION

In the book's ultimate and culminating surprise, the LORD speaks to Job out of the storm whose arrival Elihu described in his fourth speech. It turns out that this storm was not just an illustration of God's power, and not just an inspiration for Elihu, but a vehicle that was actually transporting God to the long-awaited meeting with Job. The idea of a divine being traveling on a storm fit the mythic imagination of the ancient world. But for the first time since the opening narrative, the author uses the covenant name *Yahweh* (NIV "the LORD"), to assure the Hebrew audience that this is not just a local storm god, but their own covenant God, the Supreme Ruler and Creator of the world.

The LORD confronts Job with a long series of questions. He's not trying to bully Job into submission by humiliating him with his lack of knowledge. Rather, this is another of the wisdom interrogations that are found so often in the book. But this is the first time such an extended interrogation has made up an entire speech. It has a special purpose.

In order to engage a question, a person must entertain its premises, at least provisionally. They may then answer the question directly, which requires accepting its premises. They may agree it's a valid question for which they have no answer, which also means acceptance of the premises. Or they may argue that the question isn't valid, implying that its premises themselves are flawed. But no matter how they respond, the person must first engage the questioner on their own terms. This is what the LORD is giving Job the opportunity to do.

READING

Have someone read the LORD's first speech to Job, beginning with "Who is this that obscures my plans with words without knowledge?" and ending with "Will the one who contends with the Almighty correct him? Let him who accuses God answer him!"

Then have someone read Job's brief response to the LORD.

DISCUSSION

1 When he was responding to Zophar's first speech, Job made God this offer: "Summon me and I will answer, or let me speak, and you reply to me." In other words, Job was willing to be either the defendant or the plaintiff in their court case. But he was still insisting that the case be conducted on his own terms. He asked, "How many wrongs and sins have I committed?" This, as far as Job is still concerned, is what he and God need to settle, no matter which roles they assume.

But there's a premise implicit in this question, that everything that happens in the world of humans has its origin and explanation within the world of humans. Job and his friends share this premise. They only disagree about whether a particular effect within the human world—Job's sufferings—has an appropriate cause within that world: sin and guilt on Job's part. The LORD cannot answer this question without granting this premise, which is actually incorrect. And so he chooses to summon Job to answer his own questions, which rest on a very different premise.

The LORD's wisdom interrogation begins with questions about the original creation: how the earth was established, how the seas were contained, and so forth. It then proceeds to questions about how God channels the originally chaotic forces of water through clouds and storms to nourish the earth. Finally it poses a series of questions about how various creatures can consequently survive in the wilds, finding food, giving birth, and caring for their young. The picture at the end of the interrogation is one of life thriving in intricate and varied forms beyond the domesticated world of humanity.

The implication is that the cause and explanation for things that happen within the world of humans may lie far outside that world. Eaglets, for example, "feast on blood," which is why their parents are always looking for "where the slain are." For an ancient warrior, the worst possible disgrace was to lie unburied in an open field after being killed in battle. But the LORD's questions about eagles and hawks suggest that, in a mysterious if macabre way, a person might suffer such a fate not because they were horribly wicked, but because little birds high on a distant crag need food to grow.

Job, to this point, has thought of the wilds very differently. They are a place of death: He depicts caravans going off course and perishing of thirst in the "wastelands." But the LORD describes instead how he waters those "wastelands" to make them scenes of life. For Job the wilds are also a place of desolation and disgrace, in which he feels he is now living himself, expelled from human society: "I have become a brother of jackals, a companion of owls." Job described shiftless youths on the fringes of society "braying" like donkeys. But the LORD uses the wild donkey as a symbol not of degradation, but of freedom. "It does not hear a driver's shout," he observes, echoing the exact phrase Job used to describe slaves resting in the grave.

The LORD knows that beyond the sphere of human society there's a vast realm of life, freedom, and meaning. Job has asked God, "What is mankind that you make so much of them?" In this wisdom interrogation, the LORD is effectively asking Job this same question.

⟳ When something bad happens to you unexpectedly, do you find yourself wondering, "What did I ever do to deserve this?" Or when other people suffer misfortunes, do you sometimes speculate about how they might be responsible for them? How would you think about such situations differently if you accepted the premise that the explanation for what happens in the human world may not reflect the consequences of human moral conduct, but instead serve purposes beyond the human realm?

⮑ Readers know from the opening narrative that the cause and explanation of Job's sufferings lie well outside the human realm, not even in the wilds of the untamed world, but in the councils of heaven. Job's response to his sufferings is meant to be an answer to the "problem of good." (That is, if apparent goodness is always rewarded and bad conduct is always punished, how can we ever really be sure that a person is genuinely good and not just trying to win rewards and avoid punishment? By remaining loyal to God even though he is suffering undeservedly, Job is showing that genuine good does exist.) List, if you can, some other divine purposes that might be served by things that happen to people, even if they never understand what's going on.

2 The LORD never answers Job's questions on Job's own terms ("How many wrongs and sins have I committed?"), because to do so would be to accept those terms. But the LORD does answer Job's *images*, through the language in which he poses his own questions. In this way the LORD assures Job that he has heard him and is addressing his concerns directly. Once again, simply by engaging these questions, Job must provisionally entertain a picture of the world very different from the one he has drawn himself.

Job repeatedly uses images of darkness, death, drought, inability to taste, and silence to reject life in a world that he considers capricious and unjust. The LORD has been listening all along. He responds with questions that employ images of light, birth, water, food, and sound to affirm to Job that his life has value and meaning, even if he doesn't realize it. These images counter specific ones that Job himself has used. For example, in his first response to Eliphaz, Job complained that he'd lost his appetite; food was tasteless to him. But in this speech God portrays lions and ravens and donkeys, not to mention those little eaglets, hungrily crying out for food and being satisfied.

The LORD's speech is a response in particular to Job's opening words, in which he cursed the day of his birth. Job said of that day, "May no shout of joy be heard in it . . . May its morning stars become dark." In response, the LORD describes the day of creation (Job had wished for an un-creation) as a time when "the morning stars sang together and all the angels shouted for joy." Job wished he had been like a "stillborn child," coming lifelessly out of the womb. The LORD speaks by contrast of the sea "bursting forth from the womb," full of vitality and restless energy that, when controlled and channeled, will be a source of life for the whole world. The LORD also describes how he "hedged in" (NIV "shut up") the sea. This is the same expression that Job applied to himself to complain that he was a particular target of divine scrutiny. Actually, there were much bigger players on the cosmic scene for God to restrain!

⮑ Divide your group into smaller teams and assign each team one or two of the following images: light, birth, water, food, and sound. Each team should read through the LORD's speech again and note where and how these images are used. (For example, "From whose womb comes the ice?" is a birth image; "song," "shout," "voice," and "cry" are all words that create sound imagery.) Is an image used anywhere in contrast or parallel with its opposite? Can you recognize places where the LORD uses an image to respond to something Job has said? Once the teams have finished their investigations they should share their insights with the whole group.

⮑ What images do you typically use to describe your life on earth? Are they images of affirmation or of negation? What images would God use if he were going to ask you a series of questions about your world as he does for Job here?

3 The LORD concludes his speech with an invitation for Job to answer him as if they were opposing one another in court: "Will the one who contends (*rîb*) with the Almighty correct him?" But Job declines to make any answer at all. "I am unworthy—how can I reply to you?" Job literally describes himself as small or insignificant. This is the kind of judgment expressed by the word *ma'as* (although Job does not use that specific term here, as he will after the Lord's next speech): Something is disdained as of little worth or value. Job isn't saying that he himself has no intrinsic worth but rather that his human-centered view of the world has been shown to be petty and trifling compared with the expansive panorama of wild, free created life that the Lord has sketched out through his questions. Job has engaged those questions and entertained their premises, and while he has no answer for them, he now accepts the view of the world they imply. He no longer considers himself the center of his own world and he no longer believes that his personal actions must be the cause of everything that happens to him.

↪ Is your view of the world self-centered, human-centered, or God-centered? What makes it this way? Would you like it to be any different? If so, how might it change?

↪ You go to visit Yosemite National Park and ask a park ranger as you arrive, "What's the most significant thing for me to see here?" He replies, "You're looking at him." Are you impressed?

↪ Have you ever encountered a question that you couldn't answer, but which changed your view of the world because you couldn't answer or dismiss it?

↪ Search online for William Blake's engraving of this scene, entitled "Then the Lord answered Job out of the whirlwind." (This is engraving number 13 of the ones that Blake did for the book of Job—not his wash drawing of the same subject.) Who would you say are the various characters in Blake's illustration? Do you picture the scene in a similar way, or in a different one? Invite the artists in your group to create their own illustrations and to show and discuss them.

THE LORD DESCRIBES THE TERRIBLE POWER OF BEHEMOTH AND LEVIATHAN

Book of Job > The Lord's Second Speech
Book of Job > Job's Reply to the Lord's Second Speech
Book of Job > Closing Narrative

INTRODUCTION

The Lord's first speech from the storm addressed two important concerns arising from Job's opening speech. The Lord countered *what* Job said he wanted to do—un-create the day of his birth—by depicting the glories of the creation thriving and pulsating with life. The Lord also spoke to *why* Job wished he'd never been born. Job felt that his life wasn't worth living if there was no coherence between his most deeply held beliefs and his actual experiences. The Lord showed him that his experiences were in fact coherent with a more profound and mysterious vision of the world, in which the cause and explanation of events within the human sphere may lie outside that sphere and may never be completely understood. Job responded to this first speech by admitting how limited a grasp he had of the world's workings.

But there is still one more concern from Job's opening speech that the Lord must address. There's a serious problem with *how* Job wanted to accomplish his purpose. He called on those who could "rouse Leviathan" to unleash this chaos monster against the day of his birth so it would no longer be an ordered, bounded period of time and would dissolve back into nothingness.

In response, the LORD describes two fearsome animals, behemoth and leviathan, and uses them to represent the chaos monster. He tells Job that no one should be foolhardy enough to rouse them. He asks, in effect, "Are you sure you want to turn such forces loose against my ordered creation? Once you got them started, how would you ever stop them?"

READING

Have someone read the LORD's second speech to Job, beginning with "Brace yourself like a man; I will question you, and you shall answer me" and ending with "It looks down on all that are haughty; it is king over all that are proud."

Then have someone read Job's brief response to this speech.

Finally, have someone read the closing narrative, beginning with "After the LORD had said these things to Job" and continuing to the end of the book.

DISCUSSION

1 The LORD begins this speech by raising the question of power. If Job really wants to run the world according to his own understanding of what's just and fair, even assuming that his understanding is correct, does he have the power to enforce justice? The LORD asks Job, "Would you discredit [or thwart] my justice? Would you condemn me to justify yourself?" (In other words, would Job replace the LORD's moral government of the world with his own?) If that's what he wants, then he has to show he has the power to defeat the wicked. If he can't restrain evil throughout the world, then he has no right to wish that he could determine justice instead of God.

⮑ Does the exercise of justice always require the exercise of power, whether force actually has to be used or is only threatened? Is there no way to overcome evil other than by being stronger than it? Is nonviolent resistance an exercise of force?

⮑ If God asked you the same questions he asks Job here, how would you reply to them?

2 The LORD illustrates the limitations of Job's power by describing two great beasts, which he calls behemoth and leviathan. Many interpreters believe that these descriptions are initially of the hippopotamus and the crocodile, two fearsome river creatures known from the Nile in Egypt. Simply by comparison with these, Job has to admit the limits of his own power. But the LORD then draws an even stronger contrast. Halfway through the long depiction of leviathan, after a significant transition in which the LORD warns against rousing such beasts and mentions Job's case against him, the portrait moves from realistic to mythological. Leviathan now takes on the characteristics of a fire-breathing dragon and comes to represent the chaos monster. As the speech ends, the LORD describes humans trying every weapon they have against this monster—swords, spears, arrows, stones, clubs, etc.—to no avail. Leviathan swims powerfully off into the deep unvanquished, leaving the seas "churning like a boiling cauldron" in his wake. So how does Job think he can rouse this monster but then get it to stop destroying God's creation after it has turned only one day of the year into chaos?

But even though Job believes that the chaos monster can be called upon selectively to undo specific aspects of the creation, the LORD explains that even behemoth and leviathan are not his eternal enemies, existing independently of him and forever opposed to his purposes. Rather, they are magnificent creatures of his own design and are under his power. God says that as behemoth's Maker he can "approach it with his sword," and he refers to leviathan as a "creature." "Everything under heaven belongs to me," he tells Job. The universe is not a battlefield where two opposing forces are locked in perpetual combat. Ultimately God controls everything, even forces of destruction that people are powerless to resist.

⮑ Invite the artists in your group to draw or paint behemoth and leviathan, as they imagine them based on the descriptions here.

⊃ In your own culture, if you wanted to portray how reckless and dangerous it is to flirt with forces that are opposed to God, what image would you use?

3 In his response to the LORD's second speech, Job once again acknowledges the limitations of his understanding, and he formally withdraws his case. The LORD asked whether Job wanted to discredit or thwart his justice, and Job now replies, "No purpose of yours can be thwarted." After repeating the questions the LORD asked at the start of his two speeches, Job admits that he has been getting into matters that are "too wonderful for me to know." And so he says, "I despise myself." But this is not an expression of self-loathing. Again the verb is *ma'as*. It is used here without any actual object, so its reference must be inferred from the context. The next thing Job says is "I . . . repent in dust and ashes." Dust and ashes are signs of humility and penitence. The Hebrew verb translated "repent" here means to turn from a planned course of action and take up a new course. It includes the sense that a person now regrets the former course or that the concerns that originally motivated it have been addressed. Job is saying that he is now satisfied, he is withdrawing his case, and he regrets the trouble he has caused. So what Job now "disdains" or "despises" (*ma'as*) as worthless and insignificant is his former belief that he had a case against God that he needed to pursue.

At the key transition in this speech, as the portrait of leviathan moves from realistic to mythological, the LORD asks, "Who has a claim against me that I must *pay*?" The term is the same one Elihu used when he asked whether Job thought God should *compensate* him on his own terms, since he disdained God's terms. "You must decide," Elihu told him. Job now chooses. He disdains his own previous sense of wounded entitlement, which he acknowledges was based on a limited understanding of the world, and accepts God's purposes, which cannot be thwarted and which most often can also not be fathomed by the mortal mind.

⊃ When Elihu says, "You must decide," he's speaking not only to Job, but to all readers of the book. Have you chosen? Which do you disdain, God's moral government of the universe or your own mortal ideas of how the world should work?

➲ Have you repented? Have you turned from a defiant course of action in relation to God to a course of trust? If you now see your place in the world and in relationship to God in a new way as a result of reading and discussing the book of Job, share your insights with the group.

➲ If you've chosen God for the first time in a way that will be significant for the rest of your life, ask your group to arrange an opportunity for you to share this publicly in a worship gathering or similar venue.

4 As the book of Job moves into its closing narrative, it changes from a philosophical conversation back into a simply worded tale of a man who lived long ago and far away. Readers are encouraged when they see Job restored to community and given a more blessed life in the end than he had in the beginning. The book begins with the sense of "once upon a time" and ends with an air of "they all lived happily ever after."

But did they? The LORD restores Job's fortunes and gives him "twice as much as he had before." The doubling of his flocks and herds is certainly material restitution, at least. But can anything replace the children he has lost? How could Job ever be compensated for them? This troubling question lingers in the minds of readers even after the book reaches an apparently happy ending. Some interpreters suggest an intriguing resolution to this difficulty. They note that God doesn't give Job fourteen sons and six daughters to replace the seven sons and three daughters who died, even though he's supposed to have "twice as much" in the end. But if his original children were actually still alive in some sense (and the book does speak of an afterlife in several places), then Job would indeed end with twice as many children as he started with. He may even be reunited with his lost children after his own death. However, the book only offers this as an implied possibility, leaving readers to wonder.

They may also wonder why the LORD says that the three friends have not spoken the truth about himself, as Job has, and why God actually requires the friends to offer sacrifices and ask for Job's prayers in order to avoid

THE LORD DESCRIBES THE TERRIBLE POWER OF BEHEMOTH AND LEVIATHAN punishment. The friends were unimaginative and conventional, but they never accused God of injustice or indifference the way Job did. And what about Elihu, who isn't mentioned at all? While he expressed the book's overall view in some places, in others he made wild and even contradictory claims about God. Are we to conclude that God had no problem with this?

In short, the book of Job does not neatly resolve all of the complex philosophical and theological questions it raises in such a rush at its beginning and then pursues doggedly throughout the characters' speeches. We should not expect anything different from this work that proclaims in a key central passage (the Hymn to Wisdom) that only God ultimately knows the way to wisdom, that "he alone knows where it dwells." Human investigation and reasoning can never definitively establish whether this is truly a world of order, meaning, purpose, and beauty rather than a place where people are lost in tragedy and absurdity for a few short years.

At the same time, however, the very composition of the book of Job may be an implicit claim that the world is indeed a place of order and beauty. Throughout the book we've noted how intricately it's crafted, through the repetition and variation of distinctive imagery, through verbal parallels and plays on words, through the grandeur of eloquent poetry, and through contrasts, tensions, paradoxes, ironies, and surprises. And so even as the book portrays human society and culture to be a fragile realm resting precariously within a wild and untamed creation, it draws this portrait in such a way as to suggest that the whole creation actually has the same character as the book itself: surprising, elusive, even frustrating, but ultimately very beautiful.

⮕ What would you say to someone who, after reading the book of Job, still believes that the world is more a place of tragedy and absurdity than a place of order, meaning, purpose, and beauty?

⮕ Is the act of creating art or literature a way of representing the world as having order, beauty, and meaning? In the final analysis, is the medium the message in the book of Job? In other words, are readers of Job supposed to come to a conclusion about the world not just from what the book says, but from the artistic way in which it says it? Explain why you would say yes or no.

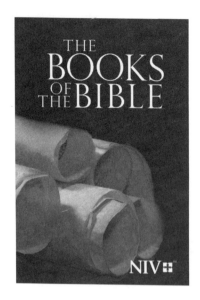
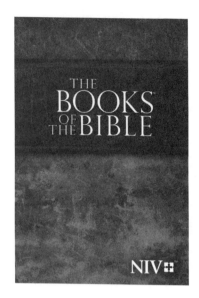

Clean. Beautiful. Unshackled.

- chapter and verse numbers removed
  (chapter and verse range given at bottom of page)
- natural literary breaks
- no additives: notes, cross-references,
  and section headings removed
- single-column setting
- whole books restored (Luke–Acts, Samuel–Kings, etc.)
- book order provides greater help in understanding

There is no Bible more suited to reading—from the beginning of the book to the end—than *The Books of the Bible*. This "new" approach is actually the original approach, and I love it.

Scot McKnight
North Park University

For more information on how to use this Bible and the UNDERSTANDING THE BOOKS OF THE BIBLE series with your whole church or small group, visit www.biblica.com/cbe.

ALSO AVAILABLE

Bible reading is declining at such a rapid rate that within 30 years the Bible will be a "thing of the past" for most Christ-followers. One of the main reasons for this decline is the format of the Bible. The format we know today was created so that a "modern" world could divide and analyze and systematize the Scriptures. But this made the word of God practically unreadable. As we move into a postmodern world, we'll need to recapture the stories, songs, poems, letters, and dreams that naturally fill the pages of Scripture. Only then will a new generation of readers return to the Bible.

Christopher Smith argues in this book that the "time for chapters and verses is over." He explains how these divisions of the biblical text interfere with our reading and keep us from understanding the Scriptures. He describes how Biblica has created a new format for the Bible, without chapters and verses, with the biblical books presented in their natural forms. And he shares the exciting new approaches people are already taking to reading, studying, preaching, and teaching the Bible in this new presentation.

Paperback, 234 pages, 5.5 x 8.5
ISBN: 978-0-8308-5600-8
Retail: $16.00

Available for purchase online or through your local bookstore.

ALSO AVAILABLE

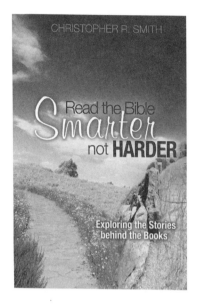

There is an increasing recognition that we need to engage the Bible as a collection of books. But we haven't been taught to read or study the Bible on the book level. Almost all of our approaches to the Bible are based on chapters, verses, or sections, so how do we change this?

The units of meaning in the Bible are not chapters, or verses, or topical sections, but the literary compositions that God inspired to create the Scriptures. If we want to know the meaning of God's Word, we need to engage these compositions on their own terms. This means understanding why they were written, what kind of writing they are, how they are put together, and what major themes and ideas they develop and pursue. This book answers these questions for each of the books in the Bible by presenting expanded versions of the book introductions included in *The Books of the Bible*, an edition of the Scriptures from Biblica that presents the biblical books in their natural literary form, without chapters and verses.

Paperback, 168 pages, 5.5 x 8.5
ISBN: 978-0-8308-5742-5
Retail: $15.00

Available for purchase online or through your local bookstore.